In Your Dreams

*Have you ever woken from a startling dream
and wondered, what does it mean?*

Zoran Paunovich

Golden Grain Publishing

In Your Dreams

The National Library of Australia Cataloguing-in-Publication information:
Paunovich, Zoran.
In your dreams : have you ever woken from a startling dream and wondered, what does it mean?

Bibliography
Printed book   978 0 9585523 9 4
eBook   978 0 9945786 3 1

1. Dreams. 2. Dream interpretation. 3. Christian life. I. Title

154.63

Published by: Golden Grain Publishing

First printing August 2003
Revised and Reprinted 2016

Dream Interpretation; Christian resource.

ENDORSEMENTS

"Dreams and visions have been prevalent in every dispensation of the Bible. Zoran has approached the subject of dreams with a prophetic passion and quest to see the church empowered and equipped with a greater understanding of this area. His research and experience, together with his sound references of Biblical truths and patterns, build a foundation of confidence upon which the reader can examine the significance and relevance of their dreams."

Russell Evans, Senior Pastor
Planetshakers Church, Melbourne Australia

"Dreams can be a powerful medium for God to communicate with us and provide direction and guidance for our lives, so knowing how to interpret dreams is a skill that every person should seek to develop. Zoran will help you understand more about the nature of dreams and how to approach their interpretation in your personal world."

Phil Pringle, Senior Minister
C3 Church Oxford Falls, Sydney, Australia

"The Language of the Holy Spirit, and the way God speaks to us, is never limited to a person's native tongue. Zoran helps us with keys to clearly recognise and understand the voice of God in the language of dreams. In doing so Zoran helps equip every believer to hear more clearly and respond more confidently. I highly recommend this book."

Martin Steel, Senior Minister
Harbourside Church, Auckland, New Zealand

"Zoran has a real passion for seeing the church grow in prophetic insight and expression. His in-depth research and personal prophetic gifting have resulted in this outstanding guide to understanding and interpreting dreams. It will inspire you to have your spiritual eyes opened afresh."

Tim Hall, Evangelist & Artist
Tim Hall International Ministries

ABOUT THE AUTHOR

Over the years, thousands of people both nationally and internationally, have benefited from hearing Zoran speak. He is widely known for his subject on dreams and visions and his understanding of the prophetic ministry.

God has used Zoran's thought provoking messages and humorous illustrative technique to bring new influence to the postmodern pulpit.

Zoran is a senior lecturer at Planetshakers College, majoring on the subjects: 'The Prophetic Life'; 'Teamwork & Leadership'; 'Pastoral Care'; and 'Communication & Preaching'.

He believes that Twenty-First Century technology must be accompanied by First Century power and impartation. He is passionately committed to preaching a Spirit-filled, Christ-honouring, life-transforming message, with the conviction of seeing people encounter the power and presence of God.

Zoran has served in three denominations over his thirty years in ministry, exposing him to a broad-based understanding of the Body of Christ. Fifteen of those years were shaped in fulltime youth ministry, giving him the ability to communicate his message to people on various levels.

Some of Zoran's popular preaching series include: 'Five Keys to Unlocking the Secrets to Your Dreams'; 'Seven Qualities to an Unshakable Faith'; 'Three Keys to a Restful Spirit'; 'The Double Portion'; 'Favour in the Furnace'; 'Gift of Friendship' and more.

Zoran was born in former Yugoslavia, lived in Italy and Sweden for five years, before moving to Australia with his family at the age of six. He now lives in Geelong, Victoria, he is happily married to his wife Kate and they have three children.

THANKYOU

To my wife Kate: You are my number one cheerleader. Your encouragement, help and support have made all this possible. You're the best!

To my three musketeers: my children, Bonnie, Amy and Michael, who have taught me that work, rest and PLAY are important.

To my mother: No gift I've ever given to you could equal the gift you have given me – life. Your sacrificial love and endurance are a constant example.

To my father: Your love and compassion for the lost and lonely will forever be a reminder to me of my purpose and mission in life.

To Meredith Resce and her team of editors at Golden Grain Publishing, who have creatively and cleverly transformed the preacher into a writer. Thank you for your patience and professionalism.

To Pastor Bruce Claridge for his spontaneous burst of creativity in coming up with the title for the book.

To the Holy Spirit who is the true author and inspiration of these pages. His goal is my goal, to make God famous by declaring Jesus Christ as King of kings and Lord of lords!

CONTENTS

In Your
Dreams

INTRODUCTION

MY PERSONAL INTEREST

I had given very little attention to dreams until the year 1985 while doing a Discipleship Training School with Youth With A Mission in Sydney, Australia. A guest speaker by the name of Herman Riffel, from the USA, taught one session on Interpreting Dreams. I had never heard of anybody who taught that God could speak to people in dreams. Immediately I bought his book, and it was to be the first of many such books that I would purchase over the years.

This man had ignited something in my spirit and I became consumed with a passion to know more and a hunger that began to motivate me. With neither pilot nor compass, I ventured out into uncharted waters, asking the Lord to help me in my quest for revelation and truth about the concept of dreams.

THE RESEARCH

It wasn't long before I realised very little material on this subject was available in Christian bookstores. Curiosity urged me to discover just how many books had been written in the area of dreams. When I spoke to the librarian at Melbourne University I was taken aback at his response. "We have 150 titles on this subject." I asked myself why, if the Bible has so much to say about dreams and visions, are there so few who are writing books from a Biblical perspective? I felt like a man who had ventured out into the Pacific Ocean rowing only a little dinghy, trying to chart my course and hoping to find something or someone who would be able to help navigate me through it.

Somewhat discouraged at the lack of Bible-based material, I began to read secular books, weeding out a great deal of nonsense as I went. It was a little like eating a regular chicken dinner where I ate the meat and spat out the bones, only here I found myself spitting out more bones than eating meat. All along I prayed and asked the Lord to direct my steps to Bible-based authors.

Thank God this situation has now changed in recent years. During the 1990's there has been more and more Christian literature on the subject of dreams written by sound authors. To my knowledge, this book will be the first Australian Bible-based production on the subject of dreams. I truly hope that it will spark interest in this subject right across the nation.

Rick Joyner, in his book, *A Prophetic Vision for the 21st Century,* states: "From the beginning, the two primary ways the Lord has spoken to his people have been through dreams and visions…however, this is probably one of the least understood subjects in the church. As we come to the end of this age, it will become increasingly essential for us to know how to distinguish dreams and visions that are from the Lord from those that are not. We must also know how to interpret them."[1]

Sadly, many misguided and misinformed people are turning to the New Age, seeking out psychics and mystics to quench their thirst for supernatural meaning to their own dreams. We know from the Bible (Deuteronomy 18:10-13) that God does not approve of such practices as consulting mediums and sorcerers, that it is not only unacceptable but dangerous as well. I passionately believe that the Holy Spirit wants to empower the church to answer the hunger that so many have for truth and revelation.

There are few subjects that attract as much interest and curiosity as this one. It is not uncommon to see several hundred people attending a Dreams seminar. I once spoke in a town with a population of around 2500 and some 300 people turned out to the seminar, with many registering a further interest in the Christian faith.

THE GOAL

It is important that we understand and echo the same attitude that Joseph had in Genesis 41:16, when summoned by Pharaoh to interpret his dream. "I cannot do it, but God will..."

It is the Holy Spirit who enables and empowers us with the ability to interpret a dream. We must always be careful to acknowledge God and make sure the credit goes to Him.

This book—a compilation of my personal experience, research and insights—is but a small contribution to the subject.

I hope for better understanding of three main things when you read this book:

- Who you are (how you see yourself);
- Who God is (how you see the Almighty);
- Who others are (how you see people).

The material in this book has been developed over many years of study, personal experience and counselling sessions. My ultimate objective is to point you to the One whom I believe holds the answer to your every question.

He has been around since the beginning of time. Many have looked to Him in prayer and sought Him for the meaning to their dreams. Down through the corridors of time, His insight, wisdom and personal contact with man have been documented and compiled into a book. This book has outlasted every other and continues to be on the list of the world's best sellers. This book is one of the oldest known to man—**The Bible.**

Author Wilda B. Tanner states: "The Bible records over seven hundred dreams and visions."[2] I truly believe the Bible to be the greatest authority on this subject. It is a treasure chest of hidden mysteries, symbolism and parables and here is one treasure hunt I encourage you to join. May the search begin!

CHAPTER 1

The Power of a Dream

"A dream not interpreted is like a letter not opened"
Talmud

The question is: is there a purpose to our dreams or are they merely non-essential meanderings of the mind? Some have dismissed dreams as being nothing more than self-induced fantasies. Some psychologists believe that dreams are simply the mind's way of releasing trivia. Others say they are merely the mind's meaningless gibberish. And there are still others who believe that we dream to release tension and explore conflicts.

There is something about the world of dreams that holds a peculiar fascination for all people. The fact that you are reading this book perhaps gives some indication of your own curiosity on this subject.

When the word 'dream' is mentioned, many of us think immediately of an idea or concept we may have thought about during our waking hours, or perhaps in terms of a goal or something we've desired to achieve.

Have you ever considered that in these times of planning and hoping, dreaming can occur not only while you are wide awake and actively conscious, but also while you are asleep?

How many creative thoughts, wonderful ideas, directions in life or maybe even a marvellous invention have you summarily dismissed and overlooked just because you thought to yourself, *Oh, it's only a dream.*

In 1940, it was the arresting dream of a twenty-nine-year-old engineer that saved Britain from the destructive attacks of German warplanes. New York Bell Telephone Laboratories' engineer, David B Parkinson, was working with a potentiometer (a device that has a swinging pen-arm that scribbles voltage on paper) when he had the following dream.

David dreamed he was in a gun pit with an anti-aircraft gun crew. There was a gun that hit an enemy plane with every shot. When he looked closer, he saw mounted on the end of the gun a potentiometer, just like the kind he was using.

When he woke, he began to seriously think about what he had dreamed until he reached an important conclusion. He reasoned that if the potentiometer could control a pen it could also control the anti-aircraft guns. Parkinson took his idea to his supervisor, who eventually discussed it with the Bell executives. Western Electric developed it and it became known as the M-9, a device that shot down 90 percent of the German V-1 planes that came over. David Parkinson was credited with turning the tide of battle in the Second World War simply by listening to his dream.[1]

Every night our dreams are building and constructing images and messages. Is it possible that our dreams could be telling us something, trying to get our attention, even pointing us in the right direction? Could we consider that God Himself is trying to communicate with us while we sleep and, in fact, could even be the very instigator of some of those dreams?

There are dreams which may contain valuable life lessons. Is it possible that what we are unwilling to acknowledge during the daytime might confront us during the night? Could it be that dreams may give us a clue to events that may occur in the future?

Almost everyone at some time or another has awakened from a startling dream, and at least for a few moments wondered what it meant. And often the residue of that dream lingers on.

For Grace Bussel it was more than just a fleeting dream. It became a living reality. The following is an account of her story.

THE POWER OF A DREAM

The weather was threatening a storm on this December day in 1876. Sixteen-year-old Grace Bussel could not have known how important a part she would play that day, a day that would go down in history.

Outside conditions were sultry despite the high wind, which violently swung the tops of the trees and sent clouds of dust scudding across the open ground. Inside the house, Grace was set to chop the basin full of dried fruit, ready for the Christmas pudding. As she worked, she shared her thoughts with her mother.

"I had a dream again last night, Mother," she said as Mrs Bussell came past. The older woman paused to listen to her daughter, glad of the excuse to rest from the flurry of cooking and overseeing the native girls at work.

"I dreamt again of a ship just outside the breakers," Grace continued, and she seemed to be gazing into the distance beyond the window. "It was just near Calgardup, a ship with sails as well as a funnel. And there seemed to be people up in the rigging, and they were waving to me as though calling me to come and help..." her voice faded off to silence and for a long moment she gazed thoughtfully through the window.

Her mother broke the silence. "What on earth would they be doing near Calgardup?" she asked, for that was treacherous coastline off Albany, Western Australia. "There's nothing there but reefs."

The pair continued in thought for a moment, before the older woman commented. "Goodness, what a day. The sea has really been driven up in a fury. I pity your ship, darling, if it comes too near Calgardup today." She smiled and looked fondly at her daughter who still stared out of the window.

Even as she spoke, she didn't know that their aboriginal stockman, Sam Isaac, was racing toward the house in search of help. Bursting into the house Sam whisked off his hat and clutched at his beard with one hand while he gasped for breath.

"A ship ma'am," he cried, his expression clearly showing the urgency of the situation.

Grace was instantly alert and almost jumped towards him. "Where?" she demanded, although she already knew and scarcely waited to hear his reply.

"Off Calgardup, Miss."

Sam's words had hardly left his mouth before Grace vanished through the kitchen doorway, calling as she ran, "My dream! My dream."[2]

The rest of the story is remarkable as both Grace and Sam Isaac rode their horses at full gallop through the sand hills and into the breakers, just as she had seen in her dream.

It was recorded in December 1876 that at the wreck of the steamer, 'Georgette', near Cape Leeuwin, a sixteen-year-old girl, named Grace Bussell, and a native stockman played a major role in saving the lives of passengers and crew by riding their horses through the angry churning surf and returning time and time again with their human burden. It was not until 1878 that Grace received the silver medal of the Royal Humane Society while the stockman was presented with the bronze medal.[3]

The ship had been carrying 58 passengers and crew. Miraculously, 50 were rescued from certain death. This was the story of a dream that came true.

HISTORICALLY SPEAKING

Throughout history there have been many, like Grace Bussell, who have testified of dreams that came true.

The well-known Greek philosophers **Plato** and **Socrates** believed in the relevance of dreams. **Hippocrates**, the great physician, described dreams as one of the most important methods for diagnosing a patient's illness. The ancient Greeks believed in a spiritual world, a world that was often revealed in their dreams.

Julius Caesar's wife, Calpurnia, dreamed that her husband was bleeding and dying in her arms. She pleaded with him to cancel the meeting with the Senate which was scheduled for the next day. Caesar acted upon her emotional advice and postponed the meeting only to be approached later by a close friend who asked him to reconsider the decision. The friend succeeded in convincing Julius Caesar that he should not be swayed by the fleeting dream of an easily excited woman. The rest, my friends, is history.[4]

For thousands of years there have been recorded instances when world leaders have been given direction from dreams. **Alexander the Great** was one such leader. When he had already made plans to conquer Jerusalem it was two dreams that caused him to change his plans quite suddenly. Alexander dreamed that he saw the high priest in robes. On that same night, the high priest of that great city also dreamed and was told in his nighttime vision to put on his robes and meet the conqueror. When the priest appeared before Alexander in his robes, just as the great conqueror had seen in his dream,

Alexander fell prostrate before the high priest, much to the dismay of his officers.[5]

Not only do we have accounts of significant dreams that have altered the course of history, as the years and centuries have progressed, various accounts show that dreams have continued to stir and even shape the destiny of men and women.

It is recorded that **George Friedrich Händel** heard in a dream the last movements of his masterpiece, *The Messiah*.[6]

Not only Händel, but also other composers received creative inspiration through dreaming. Wagner composed *Der Meistersingers* in a dream-like state. Hayden and Mozart also composed music while dreaming. It is said that Stravinsky's music was written through dreams.[7]

How many other musicians and artists have received that vital edge to their masterpiece by inspiration that has come while they have been in an open, receptive state of sleep?

Richard Bach, the author of *Jonathon Livingston Seagull*, dreamed the second half of his book some eight years after he had written the first half.

But creative genius is not restricted to the world of music and art. Science also has a great creative component, and history has shown how God, time and again, has inspired His people in important scientific discoveries.

Albert Einstein, for instance, while still an adolescent, had a dream to which he later traced back his understanding of the theory of relativity. In that dream he was riding a sled that kept going faster and faster until it approached the speed of light. The stars began to take on fantastic new patterns and colours, dazzling the rider on the sled. Einstein commented in his later years that his entire career could be seen as an extended meditation on that first dream.[8]

A. Von Kekule, a chemistry professor, understood that the molecular structure of benzene was ring-shaped, and he came to this conclusion as the result of a dream where he saw a snake biting its tail.

A dream enabled **Elias Howe** to complete the invention of the sewing machine by working out that the eye of the needle belonged near the point.

Physicist **Neils Bohr** dreamed that planets were attached to pieces of string that circled the sun. From this dream he was able to develop his theory about the movement of electrons.

It is said that **Thomas Edison**, kept a bed in his work area. Whenever he faced a problem, needed a new idea or a better way to design one of his many inventions, he would lie down and doze off, hoping that his dreams would reveal the answers to his questions.

Nobel Prize winner, **Albert Gyorgi**, made this pertinent comment: "My work is not finished when I leave my workbench in the afternoon. I go on thinking about my problems all the time and my brain must continue to think about them when I sleep because I wake up… with answers to questions that have been puzzling me."[9]

There are still more famous achievers who found the answer to a problem, or a key to success through dreams.

In the June 27, 1964, edition of the San Francisco Chronicle, champion golfer **Jack Nicklaus** sheepishly admitted that a dream had helped pull him out of a bad slump. It had given him a clue he needed to correct a problem with his swing.[10]

John D Rockefeller, the first billionaire, made a million a week in oil. He only gave away money in loose change and was only 33 years of age when he became a millionaire. It is said that at the age of 55 he became very ill with a serious disease. He lost all his hair and began to look like an old man. His stomach was so weak that all he could eat were dry biscuits and milk. Everyone was so sure he would die, that they even had a monument already prepared for him and a grave ready to receive his body. Then he had a dream. He dreamed that he did die, but he could not take any of his money along, so he decided to give it away while he was still alive. He started giving it away by the thousands, then by the millions. As he gave away his money, his health began to improve and he lived to sixty, then seventy, eighty and ninety. He was ninety-seven when he eventually died![11] John D Rockefeller discovered an important principle contained in the Bible, so much so that he was refreshed for an additional forty-two years of effective and influential living, all from a dream.

What Rockefeller learned in his dream we see outlined clearly in Proverbs 11:24-25. "One man gives freely, yet gains even more; another holds unduly, but comes to poverty. A generous man will prosper; and he who refreshes others will himself be refreshed."

There are many well-known composers whose dreams have given birth to musical masterpieces. Dreams have inspired great literature, invention, poetry and science. They have altered the course of a leader's destiny. Could it be that dreams can offer help to us in matters of personal conflict, or our search for direction and purpose in life?

SCIENTIFICALLY SPEAKING

Doctors can check the brain waves of a sleeper with an electroenceph- alograph to determine when a person is dreaming. An even simpler method used is to watch the eyes of a sleeper which will indicate when he or she is dreaming. The dreamer's eyeballs move under the eyelids because they are literally watching a picture. The words of Nebuchadnezzar in the Bible are accurate when he says: " I saw a dream." Daniel 4:18

The movement of the eyes beneath the eyelids while a sleeper is dreaming is better known as REM, an acronym for Rapid Eye Movement. Some scientists say that during sleep the conscious and the subconscious are rearranging data. However, this explanation does not cover the phenomenon that babies even in their mother's womb experience REM. It is amazing to think that babies dream in the mother's womb.[12]

One third of our lifetime is spent sleeping. Scientific studies reveal that during REM, people can dream from one to ten minutes. If we awaken during the first half of the night, the chances are that we have been engaged in relatively vague non-REM dreaming. As the night progresses, sleep gets lighter and REM periods become longer. Sometimes dreams can be over an hour in length, and can last up to 90 minutes. The longest and most important dream is usually dreamed just prior to waking.

It is said that the ancients believed the last dream of the night would be a dream of revelation.

Another interesting discovery has shown that if a person is not allowed to dream, he or she becomes mentally disturbed. This has been tested by waking the sleeper whenever the brain waves indicated the occurrence of dreaming. Similar experiments were performed with animals that also behaved in a disturbed manner when they were robbed of their dream time. We do not know exactly why, but it certainly appears that we must dream in order to be mentally and physically healthy.[13]

Some time ago some psychologists in England performed an experiment which results showed that out of some 19,000 people, 10 percent admitted to having visions.[14]

At the dream laboratory of the United States Navy in San Diego it was discovered through research that 95 percent of the dreams not written down or told within 5 minutes are forgotten.

WHY ARE PEOPLE SCEPTICAL?

In the opening introduction to my seminars I often make this comment: "I know that among our audience today we have people who fit into one of three categories. There are those who are **sceptical** (uncertain), those who are **cynical** (suspicious) and those who are **serious** (searching)."

It is not unusual to have a person approach me after a seminar and say, "I came in sceptical but I am leaving inspired. Thank you for coming."

Dreams and visions are often in the pages of Scripture and are generously strewn throughout church history as well. However, over the past few hundred years, very little attention has been given to this subject at all. The question that has to be asked is, why?

In 1968 Mortan T. Kelsey, former professor at Notre Dame Theological College and an Episcopal clergyman, launched a book on dreams titled: *God, Dreams and Revelation*. **In this book he asserts, "Finding a Christian today who pays attention to dreams is unusual."**[15]

In that same year, at a time when most of the church was silent on the subject of dreams, the Reverend John Sanford wrote a book, *Dreams: God's Forgotten Language,* **in which he emphasised the point that "every major writer in the first four centuries of Christianity regarded dreams as one way that God offered healing and guidance to mankind."** [16]

Why is it that the early Christians commonly accepted that God could speak to people through dreams and visions? This is in stark contrast to our modern era. Nowadays, if you believe that dreams contain significant messages for your life, you could easily be looked upon as one who has lost touch with reality or one who is not quite all there.

Morton Kelsey in another of his books called *Dreams: A way to listen to God,* offers some further insight. He questions what brought an end to the tradition of dreams and visions in the western world.

"In the thirteenth century, Thomas Aquinas tried to interpret the life of the church with the help of Aristotle's philosophy - the idea that the human being can experience only through sensory perception and reason. There was no place for dreams. It took about three or four centuries for this view to become totally accepted. As this happened, Christians ceased interpreting dreams. The intellectual tradition of Europe in the last four centuries has taught people to think in conceptual terms only."

Kelsey goes on to say, "When we regard our dreams seriously then we are not separating ourselves from Christian tradition, but rather we are immersing ourselves in it."[17]

Perhaps we can now see that Aristotle's humanistic philosophy based on reason and logic has taken over as the foundation of western thinking and living. It is said that Aristotle was not taken seriously in his day. All the greatest Greek minds believed in the existence of a spiritual world.

In recent decades, however, we are seeing the tide turn with an escalating interest and fascination with the supernatural. We are noticing an increased thirst for spiritual things. The 1990s saw an increased acceptance, and consequent lapse of opposition, to things of the occult, and with this there was an introduction of a broader acceptance of the spiritual world than had been experienced in the last century. Now as we emerge into the 21st Century it is gaining increasing momentum, creating a greater consciousness of spiritual matters. Newspaper and magazine advertisements reflect the thirst for spiritual things with multiple promotions for psychics, clairvoyants, tarot card readers, astrologers and the like. Where there was once a single advertisement or perhaps two, there is now a huge range to choose from. Today, people are becoming again more open to the realm of the spirit, and I am certain God will raise up the appropriate Christian ministries to meet the needs of the spiritually bereft. It is time to equip the church with an understanding of the supernatural realm and how to function in it. Dreams play an important part in this whole scenario.

CHAPTER 2

A Dream Come True

"Why does the eye see a thing more clearly in dreams than the mind while awake?"

Leonardo da Vinci

How many times have you experienced a dream that took place later in your waking life? Gillian Holloway Ph.D. refers to them as 'snapshots of the future'.[1]

In 1951 one recorded instance of a dream come true was of a woman, who knew nothing about soccer, predicting that Newcastle United would win the F.A. Cup because she had seen their victory occur in a dream.[2]

Dr W.D.F Prince, President of the Society for Psychical Research, dreamed that he was looking at the rear end of a train, which was protruding from a railway tunnel. Then, suddenly, another train crashed into it. He saw the coaches crumple and pile up, and out of the mass of wreckage came screams from the wounded. The next morning, an express, while standing with its rear at the end of the Park Avenue tunnel in New York City, was struck by the engine of a local train. The advancing locomotive ploughed into the standing train, smashing the coaches and killing and wounding many of the passengers.[3]

These are but a couple of 'snap shot' glimpses that other people have had of their tomorrows. Personally, I'll never forget the year 2000, the year that the Essendon Football Club (The Bombers) were having an invincible season. No team seemed able to break down the brilliance and pace of their play. One morning, towards the end of the football season, I awoke from a dream that the Western Bulldogs had actually defeated the Bombers in a game. To my amazement, the teams met to play each other some two weeks after the dream, and the Bulldogs became the first team to conquer the unbeatable Bombers that year. For the record, the Bombers went on to win the premiership flag, beaten only the once for the season.

I have read numerous accounts where people have dreamed of some trivial event that later took place. I once heard a woman call into a radio talk back show to say how she had dreamed NASA's phone number. She ended up calling the number that connected her to the United States, and yes, you guessed it, NASA was on line.

The question could be asked, why do people have such dreams? Can a dream have the capacity to give you a sneak preview of the future? From biblical times until the present and no doubt into the future, until the end of the age, dreams will be regarded as having prophetic value. While these sorts of dreams are not common they certainly occur.

Take for example the dream of a friend of Pastor James Ryle.

James Ryle, Pastor of Boulder Valley Vineyard Christian Fellowship (Boulder, Colorado), has written a tremendous book titled, *A Dream Come True*. In the second chapter, titled 'Why Bother With Dreams and Visions', he makes the following observation: "God speaks in dreams and visions to accomplish many of His purposes in our lives. While there are those who will doubt it, there are many more who will tell you that He does."[4]

In the opening of that chapter, a friend of James Ryle, Jack Taylor, President of Dimensions in Christian Living, tells him of a dream he had as a young evangelist.

DRESS REHEARSAL BEFORE THE MAIN EVENT

"No one had been able to get through to this old sinner for years. His dear wife had held on, hoping that the Lord would save his soul before he died, but she had seen preachers come and go with little influence upon her hardened husband.

The night before the young evangelist was to call upon the old man and his hopeful wife, he had a dream. He saw himself at their home, sitting in the family room visiting with them. He asked, 'May I have a glass of water?'

The husband said, 'Sure I'll get it for you.'

In the dream the young evangelist saw himself follow the old man to the kitchen. As the two stood chatting, the evangelist said, 'You have two of the most beautiful daughters I have ever seen, it's very obvious that you love them.'

The old man lit up with pride. 'Yep, you sure got that right, preacher.'

Then in the dream the young man saw himself say, 'It's really too bad that you can't give them the one thing that they need the most.'

'And exactly what would that be?' the man indignantly replied. The evangelist looked the man right in the eye and answered, 'A Christian father!'

To the amazement of the preacher the man gave his life to Christ right there in the kitchen. Then the dream ended.

The next day the evangelist made the house call. As he sat in the living room visiting with the family, he decided to put his dream to the test.

'May I have a glass of water?' he asked, and just as he had dreamed, the husband had offered to get it for him. Faith arose in his young heart as he followed the old man into the kitchen. Like an actor performing a script, the young evangelist guided the conversation exactly as he heard it in the dream. When the old man asked what it was that his children needed the most that he couldn't give them, the young evangelist answered, 'A Christian father.' The force of these words visibly shook the father. He could not escape from the conviction of the Holy Spirit. There, standing in his kitchen, the old sinner repented and gave his heart to Jesus Christ - just as it happened in the dream the night before!"[5]

What a wonderful example of how God can touch a life.

WITHOUT THE SPRING THERE IS NO RING

I couldn't help but reminisce over the young evangelist's story. I too found myself living out a dream in waking life, as if it were a script. It was not long after I'd started in the ministry when I had the dream.

I dreamed several lads were sitting around me on a lawn, their pushbikes next to them. It seemed they were waiting for me to speak to them. I said to one of the lads. "Take that bicycle bell off for me." Holding the bell securely in the palm of my hand, I unscrewed the lid, opened the top and pulled out the spring from among the components. I showed the lads the spring in my hand. I said to them, "without the spring there is no ring." I went on to say that the spring is like Jesus. You can have all the components of your life together, but if you don't have Jesus (just like the spring) you will never know what it means to have that ring in your life. You'll never know what it means to have that spring in your step. No Saviour, no sound. No Jesus, no skip, no bounce, always lacking purpose and direction.

Two weeks later I received a call from a pastor in a northern Adelaide suburb asking if I would come and speak at one of his church's youth meetings. I had never met this man before, or even heard of his church. I wasn't even familiar with the suburb. I accepted the invitation and that Saturday night took along some young people from our own church. The church was an old traditional church building, with stained glass windows and wooden pews. The minister came and introduced himself, and said he couldn't stay but invited us to feel right at home. Well, there we were. I had arranged with my sister that she would lead some songs and give a solo item or two. The musicians who'd come with us finally set up their equipment.

NO ONE SHOWS UP

It was approximately 7:20pm, only ten minutes before the meeting was due to start, and there was not a soul around other than my own team. Even the minister had gone. But then I had a moment of hope that all was not lost as I looked out the rear door and saw three dark figures approaching. "Finally!" I said to myself. "At least we have three young people." But the discouragement quickly returned when I realised that the three figures were three elderly people. I did a quick check of my attitude, and hurriedly thanked God for them, but in truth I'd expected I would be speaking to young people. Somewhat dejectedly, I looked through the two glass doors on the side of the building that faced the road, and I noticed some BMX bicycles outside the corner milk bar store. I allowed the thoughts to cross my mind; *tonight is going to be one boring show unless someone turns up.* It was then that I made up my mind to do something about the situation. I made my way across the road to invite whoever I could find in the store to the meeting.

As I opened the shop door, I saw about eight young guys playing pinball.

"Hey!" I said. "We're having a meeting across the road, a youth rally. Would you like to come? What do you say?"

I omitted to tell them that the 'youth' rally was actually three senior saints, but I did let them know that we'd travelled quite a distance to be there. Well, it was only a 30-minute journey, but I had to make it sound good. I was fast approaching the point where I would be prepared to pay them to come.

Though I looked hopeful, I never got so much as boo for a reply. Somewhat despondent, I made my way back to the church, my sister started her song leading and I stood there thinking; *no minister, no young people, except the ones we brought, and a cheer squad of three elderly saints. What am I doing here?*

IS THIS AS GOOD AS IT GETS?

I had been speaking for about fifteen minutes when suddenly, the two double doors at the side of the church flung open and three lads rode into the church on their BMX bikes. They assembled at the back of the church hall and proceeded to pedal their bikes while I was speaking. I couldn't believe it. Being young and full of zeal, I desperately tried to apply all the wisdom that had been told to me. I remembered that when a distraction came up during preaching, I was supposed to keep focused and not be swayed. So I kept right on preaching, trying to pretend that nothing was going on. But this pretence became even harder when one of the lads began to do a 'mono', back wheel on the ground and front wheel and handle bars in the air. Even as I tried desperately to ignore him, I could tell he was having the time of his life. Anybody would have thought the circus had come to town.

THE DAY I PREACHED FROM THE BACK OF THE CHURCH

Eventually, it all got too much, and I thought to myself; *well if you can't beat them, join them.* I excused myself from the meeting and began to make my way through the small band of listeners to where the lads were.

"So you think this is funny?" I said, perhaps failing to hide the annoyance that I felt. "You think you're so macho that you can do what you like, where you like, and when you like. I'm going to ask you to put your bikes aside, sit down and listen to someone who has something decent to say."

Then the stakes were raised a little as I noticed the rest of the group of boys, peering in through the side doors, looking to see the entertainment that was going on inside. Some sort of daring came over me as I turned to them also, and said much the same thing. What came over me I don't know, but I challenged them to join their friends, and sit down to listen to what I had to say.

To my amazement not only did the three from the back of the church put their bikes aside and sit down, but their friends also came inside and joined them.

NOW WHAT?

"Now what?" That's exactly what I thought. "Great, what do I do now, Lord?" It's all very well to be full of bravado, but what happens when they respond and are sitting there waiting for the 'decent' thing you have to say. I continued to pray silently to myself. Then, out of nowhere I remembered the dream I'd had two weeks earlier. With all the antics, with the poor show of audience, and then the bike show at the back of the church, the dream had been the furthest thing from my mind.

But now that it crossed my mind, it came back clearly. Just like a pre-rehearsed performance, there they were, all sitting around me, waiting to hear from this crazy preacher what it was that was so important. They'd only seen the beginnings of weird, and were yet to find out just how strange I really could be as I asked one of them to take the bell off his bike. When it was handed to me, I unscrewed the lid and pulled out the spring. Word for word I began to preach the script as I had dreamed it. "Without this spring there is no ring." I felt so stupid, wondering what these guys must be thinking.

At the conclusion of my unusual presentation, I walked over to the other side of the room and extended the invitation for anyone who'd like to receive Christ into their lives to respond. Five out of the eight, including the ringleader, walked over and I prayed and introduced them to the Saviour. My group of supporting friends and personal cheer squad of three senior citizens certainly had something to celebrate.

Many stories like this one confirm that God is seriously interested in using dreams to speak to His people. In just over twenty-two years as a Christian I can only recall having two of these experiences. They may not happen regularly but when they do, there is no doubt the Lord is clearly speaking in regard to a matter of real importance.

WHAT DOES THE BIBLE HAVE TO SAY?

We know from Scripture and from personal experience that God may choose to speak to us through any method He so desires. There is no doubt that He is creative in his chosen methods of communication. On one occasion He spoke to a disobedient prophet (Balaam) through a donkey. Now the donkey is known for its stubbornness, so perhaps this was an appropriate creature to use for a prophet who refused to listen.

On other occasions angels have been sent, and while they often frightened the life out of the characters they visited, they were none the less a very effective means of communicating the thoughts of the Almighty.

At times God has spoken through his prophets and the prophetic word, and at other times He's used circumstances to get the general idea through to his people. He has used ordinary people to speak words of wisdom, as in the case where Jethro confronted his son-in-law, Moses, with a situation that needed immediate attention. Jesus often spoke to people through parables, and His message was strongly conveyed as they witnessed the working of miracles and signs and wonders.

God may choose to speak to you in any number and variety of ways, but let's make no mistake about it; He is equally as likely to speak to us through dreams.

It is important to mention that we don't take our whole direction and guidance from dreams. This is just one of many avenues that God may use to speak to your life, and it is not a substitute for reading the Bible and seeking God out in your personal prayer and devotions. However, in saying this, I also see the realm of dreams as one of the most misunderstood and neglected areas of guidance in the Christian life.

You only have to be familiar with just a few of the best known Bible stories before you begin to see a pattern emerging. Some of the major events in the Bible were strongly influenced by dreams. In the book of Matthew alone there are five instances where as a result of a dream, important Biblical figures were given guidance and safety.

Take Mary and name the child Jesus – Matt 1:20-21

Flee to Egypt with Mary and the child - Matt 2:13-15

Return to the land of Israel - Matt 2:19-21

Dwell in the town of Nazareth - Matt 2:22-23

Pilate's wife tells him to have nothing to do with Jesus - Matt 27:19

She suffered greatly in a dream because of Him.

From Genesis to the book of Revelation the Bible is like an art gallery of illustrations deriving from various dreams and visions. Any one of us can examine its pages carefully and explore the ideas and insights they contain.

The following are further examples of God speaking to people in a dream:

Abraham - God speaks to him about his great reward, his son - Genesis 15:1-21
Abimelech - warned by God in a dream - Genesis 20:3
Jacob - dreams of a ladder reaching heaven -Genesis 28:12
Laban - warned by God to be careful – Genesis 31:24
Joseph – dreams of his calling and future rule - Genesis 37:5
Pharaoh - 7 sleek/fat cows & 7 lean/ugly cows - Genesis41:1
Moses - God stands up for Moses – Numbers 12:6
Gideon - overhears dream/victory over Midianites - Judges 7:13
Samuel - as a boy hears His voice calling - 1 Samuel 3:1-3
Solomon - The Lord said to ask whatever you want - 1 Kings 3:5
Nebuchadnezzar - reveals the future and his pride - Daniel chapters 2 & 4

WHAT OTHERS HAVE HAD TO SAY ABOUT DREAMS AND VISIONS

"God reveals Himself in prophecy, in visions, and in dreams, as the Scriptures repeatedly testify. With the outpouring of the Holy Spirit, all believers, without distinction of gender, age, and social status, receive the wisdom and ability to know God."[6]

Simon J. Kistemaker from his exposition of the Acts of the Apostles

"Prophecy, visions, and dreams; the three principal forms assumed by the Holy Spirit under the old covenant, are exalted in character and united as a whole, when under the new covenant, the Holy Spirit enters into the heart, and dwells in it."[7]

John Peter Lange from the Gospel according to John

"The use of dreams and visions in the Bible seems consistent with the manifest nature of God. Throughout the Scriptures, God is declared as revealing Himself and making His ways known through chosen men."[8]

J. M. Lower, The Zondervan Pictorial Encyclopaedia of the Bible

"Some have dismissed dreams and visions as being nothing more than a self-induced fantasy. This attitude reveals both the arrogance and the ignorance of those who hold to it. To think that dreams and visions have no meaning or relevance is impertinent in light of both Biblical and church history."[9]

James Ryle, "A Dream Come True"

"We must take care that we do not neglect heavenly monitions through fear of being considered visionary; we must not be staggered even at the dread of being styled fanatical, or out of our minds. For to stifle a thought from God is no small sin"[10]

Charles Spurgeon, in a sermon about a dream he had.

CHAPTER 3

Why Do we Dream?

"The most notable impulse which I ever experienced happened during a dream"

John Newton, Author of *Amazing Grace*

"Do all dreams come from God?"

People often ask me this question. Though I am persuaded that some dreams do, not everything we dream comes from God. Whether from God or not I have often found many dreams to be inspirational and instructive. I am of the opinion that dreams can be categorised into two areas. They can either be: supernatural or natural. Perhaps we should consider a third category of pizza, pasta and Coke induced.

I have looked at Ecclesiastes 5:3 from four different translations that I believe sheds some light on dreams and their possible source.

"For a dream comes from much *effort...*" – NAS
"As a dream comes when there are many *cares...*" - NIV
"For a dream comes through a multitude of *business...*" - NKJ
"For a dream comes with many *concerns...*" - MLV

In these interpretations of the original, the translators have found four aspects in the same phrase, which help us to understand why we might dream. Natural dreams are not necessarily spiritual dreams. Natural dreams are a sorting out and arrangement of the day's events, activities, general business, cares and concerns, by the brain which are often recalled after we wake.

Perhaps there has been an unresolved conflict that has taken place at work. The kind of dream that might indicate this could be of a person in bed with their work clothes on, which would suggest that they have taken their work life home.

A friend of mine dreamt that his warehouse was on fire. I already knew him to be a workaholic, and felt immediately that the warehouse in the dream symbolised his work life. It seemed as if the dream was a warning for him to slow down or burn out.

Many times we do not listen to our friends' counsel or our body's warnings and so when we do not respond to issues during the day, the inner problem confronts us during the night in the form of a dream.

Jane and Tom Hamon pastor the International Family Church in Santa Rosa Beach, Florida, USA. In Jane's book *Dreams and Visions*, she makes a pertinent comment in reference to natural dreams.

"Not all dreams contain revelation from God. When we are awake, not all of our thoughts are God's thoughts running through our mind. Likewise, when we sleep, the natural mind continues to process natural thoughts."[1]

WISHFUL THINKING

Author Geoffrey A. Dudley writes that some of our dreams can be nothing more than mere wishful thinking. A dream can be the open or disguised expression of a wish.

For example, a single girl of thirty stated, "I am often dreaming I am back at the bank where I used to work. I realise now I should've stayed at the bank." She added, "I often wish I were back."

The wish that is expressed in a dream may be either conscious or unconscious; that is to say, the dreamer may or may not be aware of it. In the above example the dreamer was aware of her wish, which can therefore be called a conscious dream. At other times, however, the dreamer is not aware of a wish as being the basis of a dream.

When a person dreams that he is drinking a cool glass of water, he may wake up and find that he is thirsty. For instance, the explorer, Mungo Park, recorded the time he was journeying through Africa and the things he dreamed of. Apparently his dreams were consistently about the well-watered hills and valleys of his home. The fact that there were times when he was nearly dying of thirst leads us to suppose that the desire to quench his thirst translated itself during his sleep into this particular dream.[2]

Wishful dreams such as these have little to do with anything supernatural, and help us to remember that not every dream is necessarily relevant to any particular real-life situation or decision. As you continue with this book, you will see many references and examples of both natural and supernatural dreams.

SEVEN REASONS WHY WE DREAM

I believe the Lord uses the realm of dreams to draw our attention to all kinds of life considerations. The following seven aspects of dreaming may further help us to understand.

1. Dreams can reveal deep-seated conflicts that affect our everyday lives.
2. Dreams can provide us with insight into our own motivations and feelings.
3. Dreams can provide God's answers to our questions.
4. Dreams can warn us of impending danger.

5. Dreams can be God's way of keeping us from pride.
6. Dreams can be what God uses to get our attention when we are not listening.
7. Dreams can reveal the future.

Let's look at each reason in depth:

1. DREAMS CAN REVEAL DEEP SEATED CONFLICTS THAT AFFECT OUR EVERYDAY LIVES

Dreams can be a reflection of some inner turmoil that we are going through, whether it is a personal conflict or some relational difficulty, at work or home, with our spouse, workmate or children. If such conflict or anxiety lies hidden from view it is likely to express itself eventually in one form or another. Dreams are often a common expression for this kind of stifled anxiety.

I wonder how many times you have wrestled with the inability to measure up to personal expectations or standards imposed by others.

I remember a particular time of frustration; I was feeling as if I were in no-man's-land in respect to my involvement in church ministry. I looked at some of my colleagues who were progressing nicely, some younger than myself, which made it all the more frustrating. It was here I began to wonder what would ever become of my life. No doubt I'm not the only one who has found themselves battling this sort of frustration, still, as time went on it became more of an issue in my life and was what I believe led to the following dream:

THE WAITING ROOM

I dreamed I was in a doctor's waiting room, and it seemed that I was waiting there forever and a day. The room was full of other people waiting for their name to be called. A minister that I knew, who was younger than I, had just walked in, but wasn't there more than a minute before his name was called. I was deeply annoyed as I felt that this was most unfair. And then I woke up.

While considering some dreams I take time to pray for an understanding or interpretation, but on this occasion the dream was quite straightforward. It was obvious to me that the dream was a reflection of the way I was feeling at the time. The dream was reassuring me that even though it seemed that it was my turn, it was not yet my time for a change in the direction of my life. I felt God reassure me that I need not get frustrated, and that my turn would come. But for now all I needed to do was just wait and not get bothered by the opportunities that came up for others before my own opportunity came.

ALL CUT UP

A father shared this troubling dream with me. In his dream he saw his son's body in a coffin. It had been cut up into pieces, as though it had been through an egg-slicer. He turned around to see his wife beginning to faint and he caught her in his arms, then fell backwards into the coffin landing on top of his son's dead body.

The father, who served as a Christian minister, was concerned about his son's lack of interest in Christian matters. The young man had a girlfriend who did not share the family's Christian faith, which added to the concern. As a pastor he was concerned how all this might appear to his congregation, as he realised he was leading the church and yet struggling to lead a member of his own family. He wrestled with thinking himself unfit to pastor, the church. He imagined what his congregation might be thinking, and it all bothered him greatly. But in it all, he loved his son dearly. The son was not very responsive to his father and the relationship between them was often strained and tense.

After praying about it, this is what I believe the dream meant: The minister's approach in dealing with his son was 'cutting his boy up'. His son's death and consequent laying in the coffin were symbolic of the boy's deadness in response to him. In the dream, where the father finds himself catching his fainting wife, his wife represents the nurturing and sensitive side of his life which, in this case, was tired and low on tolerance; that is the father was emotionally exhausted in his dealings with his son. The dream seemed to be a warning that if he continued constantly harassing the boy he would find himself in the coffin with his son, his fatherly affections for his son snuffed out.

When I ventured this interpretation, the minister agreed that it was an accurate description of how he was feeling and the way he was handling the situation. Together we prayed and committed his son to the Lord's care. The father became hopeful that the girlfriend might become a Christian, which perhaps would influence the son towards turning back to his Christian family and upbringing.

As it turned out, the next day the young lady came to join us for lunch. During her time with us, I was able to shed light on a dream that she had had, and that afternoon she decided to become a Christian. How awesome are His ways, if we will only learn to trust Him!

God can use a dream to help guide us and show us certain things in respect to our internal conflicts and deep-seated hurts. On many occasions if we listen to these types of dreams we will discover the wisdom they hold for our lives.

2. DREAMS CAN PROVIDE US WITH INSIGHT INTO OUR OWN MOTIVATION AND FEELINGS

I know a man in his latter years who so disliked his father that it verged on hatred. I tried to do all I could to encourage him to reconcile with his father. Then one Sunday evening, a visiting minister to our church began to pray for this man, not having any idea of his background or who he was. The minister began to pray saying, "You know, God is your Father. He loves you and deeply cares about your life. You may never have known what it means to have a father. You may have felt fatherless, but God is encouraging your life. He's your father and cares for you."

It was not a complex or complicated prayer but seemed to be exactly what he needed to hear. It was a moment of tremendous healing and serious reflection over his years with his father. At that point, I thought he would now be able to sort things out with his dad, but it was actually more complicated than I had thought. Obviously they had grown poles apart in their relationship together.

THE HEADLESS FATHER

God's desire is that we enjoy life and the relationships we have with each other. I wasn't surprised then, that God wasn't about to give up on this man. He had a dream one night and casually mentioned it to me. As he described the dream as weird, and that it was about his father, my interest was piqued and I listened carefully as he began to speak.

"I dreamt I was in a park and my father was giving me a swing. I was having a good time, until I realized he was headless."

As weird as the dream was I felt it was very significant for him. What man who despises his father would dream of such a happy moment with his dad? That the father should be headless made it all the more unusual.

As I prayed, the Holy Spirit began to reveal to me that the dream was identifying how the man really felt about his dad. Cheerfully allowing his father to swing him was drawing the curtains back, revealing his true feelings towards his father and his deep unacknowledged desire for reconciliation. The headless father in the dream was an encouragement to him to approach his dad without worry of any *head-on* confrontation.

Again I urged him to pursue reconciliation with his father, and some days later I was pleased to hear that he had done just that. He had approached his father and was surprised to see how friendly his dad was towards him.

Dreams can reveal the true state of our feelings and motives no matter how hard we try to conceal them. As we respond to truths revealed in dreams, we can work toward the freedom and joy that can be found in living life the way it was meant to be lived. A favourite verse of mine from the Bible found in Galatians 5:1 says, "It was for *freedom* that Christ set us *free*. Stand firm, then, and do not let yourselves be burdened..."

The purpose of dream interpretation should always be to see people released from burdens such as anxiety, bitterness, fear and the like, and to work toward seeing people live free of those things. At no time should anyone accept an interpretation that leads to accepting any of this sort of burden, including confusion and condemnation. The purpose of a God-given dream is to reveal truth. The Bible says it best in the gospel of John 8:32: "Then you will know the truth and the truth will set you free."

THE DREAM OF CHARLES HADDON SPURGEON

I first heard of this dream from a visiting preacher who spoke of it one Sunday morning in the early 80s.

C.H. Spurgeon was known in his day as the prince of preachers. In his time he was also known for having a church of 6000 people. He was doing well in his chosen work; the organisation he ran was thriving. It would have been easy for a man in his position to think that his life needed little attention. It was one night in the life of Spurgeon that changed all the days to follow.

HOW IS YOUR ZEAL?

"In my dream someone opened the door and came in. His countenance showed benignity, weight of character and intelligence. He addressed me by asking, 'How is your zeal?' He could not have asked a question which gave me more pleasure to answer, for at that particular time the Lord was blessing the ministry, to the salvation of souls, my office-bearers were working harmoniously, and the finances of the church were good.

He said 'Give it to me.' Immediately I conceived it to be a physical quantity and put my hand into my bosom, and plucking it out, gave it to him. He put it into a crucible (which he carried with him), and set it on fire. After he had fused it he took it off the fire and allowed it to cool. He took it out of the crucible, and then I saw it had resolved itself into different layers or strata. He took a hammer and broke it into pieces, separating all the different parts, analysing them as to their elements, and taking notes all the time. After he had completed his investigations, he handed me the paper, and with a very sad face said, 'May the Lord save you.'

I took the paper and read -

Candidate For A Crown Of Glory

Weight of Zeal in the mass - 100 lbs gross, of which on analysis there proved to be :-

Personal Ambition	*25 parts*
Love of Power	*25 parts*
Pride of Denomination	*23 parts*
Bigotry (narrow minded)	*20 parts*
Love of Man	*4 parts*
Love of God	*3 parts*

Spurgeon went on to say:

"Immediately I felt disposed to dispute the correctness of the analysis, but my mysterious visitor had withdrawn himself, and all that I heard as he left was a deep groan. I sank upon my knees and looked again at the paper; it had become a looking glass in which I read my own heart and found that everything written in that paper was true. If in former years I had prayed, 'Lord save me from sins,' my prayer that day was ten times more earnest, 'Lord save me from myself.' And if in later years my ministry has been more marked by the absence of these unworthy motives, under God, I owe it to the visit of that mysterious stranger, whom I hope to meet above."[3]

It makes you wonder if our own heart were to be put on the scales whether we too might be found wanting. Perhaps it would cause us to be honest with ourselves. Perhaps we would find more time for the important things in life, like family and spouse. Integrity would find new meaning, as would honesty and genuine love for God and our fellow man. I wonder what would happen if you were to have a heavenly visitor do a stock take of your life. How would the report card read?

HAVE A NICE DAY

Dreams have a way of bringing out the real you. If you pay attention to the message for your life you will keep on growing spiritually and emotionally. They have the ability to spur you on with their uplifting messages.

Take this dream for example. It really made my day and the day hadn't even started. It was as if the message of this dream was, "Have a nice day, you're doing OK."

HOW'S THE HOUSE?

That particular night I dreamt that visitors had called unexpectedly. Despite being quite surprised, I invited them in. They asked if I could show them around. I remember being surprised at the wonderful design and decor of the place. It seemed to be split-level. I took them from one room to another and they marvelled as I did. The visitors asked how many squares the house was and I answered that it was thirty squares. They went on to ask if they could see the outside, and as we went about outside, it too was wonderful, with the landscaping, shrubs and lawns all tidy and complementing each other. Upon leaving they thanked me and again said how delightful and tidy the place was. As I walked back inside, thoroughly encouraged by their words, I felt disappointed that I didn't have a fourth bedroom.

Upon waking I immediately felt the Lord's favour on the dream. It was plain to me that the house represented my life. The home was in good order both inside and out (spiritually and physically). I understood 30 squares to be periods of time. It seemed to fit, as I had only just celebrated my 30th birthday. The dream was very encouraging and uplifting. The lack of a fourth room was a reminder not to get too proud or complacent, and that there is always more room for growth.

KEEP THE GROWING GOING

Each of us should have a strong commitment to personal growth and development. It would be tragic to reach fifty years of age and only have attained thirty squares. In my earlier years I was easily intimidated by those who were older. However as I looked more closely at their lives it became apparent that some of these people had made little or no progress even after several years. When they talked of their ten or twenty years' experience I could see that some were forty or fifty years of age but had only twenty squares of growth and development.

There is something in all of us that says, 'I'm tired of being the same old size, each year doing the same old things, with the same old results'. It's a desire to grow, and if you haven't already, now is a good time to develop an appetite for expansion and growth; a time to challenge yourself to new exploits. Make a solid commitment to your personal growth and expansion. Keep seeking and searching. Most of us spend plenty of time and attention feeding our stomachs. How much more should we develop a routine that will equally nourish our mental, emotional and spiritual selves? I once heard Jim Rohn say, "I pity the man that has a favourite restaurant and does not have a favourite thinker."[4]

Dreams such as these can greatly encourage and motivate us to further growth by the expanding of the horizons in our life. I was also at peace knowing that my house was in order with God and man. It is important to note that often when we dream of a house it refers to our personal life. As for me, it's now 50 squares and growing. How about you?

3. DREAMS CAN PROVIDE ANSWERS TO OUR QUESTIONS

It was in the winter of 1985 as I was coming to the end of my Discipleship Training School at Youth With A Mission in Sydney. I was praying and asking the Lord whether I should leave Australia, my family and friends, and go to what was then called Yugoslavia to be a missionary to my own people. I needed to know whether it was what the Lord wanted for my life or whether it was just an idea in my own mind. Before going to bed that night I prayed, asking the Lord for direction, desperately wanting to know whether my request was a God idea or my own good idea.

SHALL I GO TO YUGOSLAVIA?

That night I dreamt I was in Yugoslavia in a typical European home. I saw the gardens, fruit trees, and stone paved paths. I found myself in the kitchen seated at the end of a long timber table. It was long enough to seat about eight people. However, apart from myself, there were only three, seated together at the other end of the table.

These distinguished looking gentlemen all appeared the same, dressed in three-piece suits, wearing beards and ties. All three of them came across to me as though they were ambassadors, talking to me telepathically. They asked me in Yugoslav, "What's on your mind?" I told them about my uncertainty as to whether I should go to Yugoslavia to be a Missionary or not. They turned to one another as though consulting about my question. Simultaneously they turned to look at me as though with an answer. "What you're asking is a good thing, though it's not the right thing," was their reply. And so ended the discussion and the dream.

This was one of those supernatural dreams. It was clear to me from my understanding of the Bible, that the three distinguished gentlemen in the dream were the Father, Son and Holy Spirit in consultation about my life. They looked like triplets. The Scriptures came quickly to my mind. There are only two references in the entire Bible that I can find where the three came together in counsel.

Genesis 1:26 "Then God said, let Us make man in our image in our likeness…"

Genesis 11:7 At the tower of Babel "Come, let Us go down and confuse their language so that they will not understand each other."

I might take a moment to say that I was awestruck at the thought that the Godhead would come together in counsel over my prayer. I hope that this dream can be a source of encouragement to you too as you seek out God's answers to your questions. The dream helped me understand my value and importance to God and His purpose being out worked in my life.

Jürgen Matthesius is the Youth Pastor at Christian City Church, Sydney, and is known nationally and internationally as a particularly effective youth communicator. While having lunch with Jürgen, he began to relate the following dream he'd had. Jürgen was at the crossroads of life and unsure whether to pursue a certain secular career or go to Bible College. He began to question and pray about how he was going to support himself financially and see all that he owed was paid. The following dream became instrumental in his decision-making.

WHICH WAY? LEFT OR RIGHT?

Jürgen told me that in his dream he was driving a car. He pulled up at an intersection with his right indicator on. He came to a complete stop though the traffic light was green. At the intersection was a sign pointing right with Bible College written on it.

The day following the dream he'd told a girl he knew, about it. She told him the dream was indicating that it was *right* for him to go to Bible College. The car was symbolic of his own life that came to a stop, though he was given the green light and the sign to go ahead with Bible College. His approach to the decision was one of caution and hesitation, wondering which way to turn.

The young lady showed great insight when interpreting this dream. This was obviously the Holy Spirit using a dream to reassure Jürgen of his destiny.

SWEET NOW, SOUR LATER

A friend of mine was deliberating over a certain decision she needed to make. She had a dream in which she bought a chocolate éclair. As she made her way out of the shop, she sank her teeth into it, but then noticed the receipt docket. Suddenly she felt sick realising she had just paid $1000.00 for it.

When I asked her what she felt the dream meant, she said, "I knew that if I went ahead with the decision that it might be sweet at first, but it would cost me dearly later."

My time as a staff member at the church in Geelong had come to a close. After six years of service the Lord had clearly shown me that as a family we were to move to Bendigo, Central Victoria, and I would begin as the associate to the senior minister. I wrestled with the thought of going to a smaller church. I foolishly began to compare myself with some of my colleagues who had moved on to larger churches. This became more and more of an issue as I was contemplating whether or not to go. It perhaps seems strange that I should debate the issue when I knew for certain the Lord had said to go. Yet I was concerned that a smaller environment would frustrate me.

Approximately two days later, a friend of mine came to tell me about a dream she'd had. This friend is a devout woman whose prayer life and devotion to the Lord I greatly respect. Now, you have to remember I was struggling with the thought of moving on to a smaller church - the emphasis being *small*.

ROOM TO MOVE

She said to me: "I had a dream about you Zoran. It means nothing to me, but I can't help thinking that it may be of significance to you. I saw you sitting behind a desk busily writing away. You were in a small room. There was a tremendous light that filled the room. It had a great intensity to it and was very bright. The room started off small and steadily grew and grew and grew until it became a large room. Does that mean anything to you?"

I didn't need to be a rocket scientist to realise that the dream was confirming that I was going to a smaller church to begin with, but given time it would grow. The desk merely reflected that the dream was associated with my working environment. The light can only mean the Lord's presence and hand of favour that would be with me.

4. DREAMS CAN WARN US OF IMPENDING DANGER AND WRONG DOING

We would do well to pay attention to dreams that seem to warn us of danger. Perhaps there is something practical we can do to prevent trouble, or maybe it is simply a matter of getting down on our knees and praying. Take for example my sister's response to the situation following a dream she had.

She had dreamed that both our parents had been involved in a serious car accident. Though she woke up troubled by the dream, she eventually dismissed it as unlikely, and went about her normal routine.

Imagine her dismay, when several days later she found out that there had been an accident involving both our parents, and that both were lucky to be alive. The car had rolled, glass shattered and metal dented, and my father had struggled to free my mother from the wreck, fearful that with a full tank of fuel it would erupt in flames.

My sister felt considerable remorse that she had not acted on the dream, at least by praying for their protection.

Such dreams are quite common, but rather than becoming fearful, I would encourage the dreamer to take it as a cue to pray immediately for the person they've dreamed of. A phone call to say 'I'm thinking of you,' may prove useful, unless there is a strong urge from the Holy Spirit to take other action.

ALMOST ADULTERY

A certain king had ignorantly taken the wife of another man. She was very beautiful, and unaware that she was married, his intentions were obvious. That evening when the king retired to his bedroom the unexpected happened. God visited the king in a dream. We can pick up the story in the Bible, Genesis 20:3

'God came to King Abimelech in a dream one night and said to him, "You are as good as dead because of the woman you have taken; she is a married woman."'

In the dream the king defended his actions, declaring his innocence. God answered his appeal by saying, "Yes, I know you did this with a clear conscience, and so I have kept you from sinning against me. That is why I did not let you touch her. Now return the man's wife for he is a prophet, and he will pray for you and you will live. But if you do not return her, you may be sure that you and all yours will die."

I doubt the king went into any further dialogue, as the instructions were quite clear. After all, it was God who was speaking. Even the king realised that you can mess with anyone you like in this world, but don't mess with the Living God. I wonder whether the king got any sleep that night.

When the king went on to return Abraham's wife to him, he had some strong words to say. Here is one instance where God used a dream to prevent a man from doing wrong and having to face the consequences.

NIGHTMARE ON DEATH ROW

Here is another example of how a man didn't heed a warning and should have.

Pilate was sitting on the judge's seat ready to pass sentence on a prisoner called Jesus, king of the Jews. In burst an official with a note from his wife. "Don't have anything to do with that innocent man, for I have suffered a great deal today in a dream because of him." Matthew 27:19

Upon reading this, Pilate proposed the release of a prisoner as a show of Roman kindness. He gave the Jews a choice: Jesus or Barabbas. He seemed to think this was a way to have Jesus released and relinquish all responsibility. He never imagined for a moment they would choose Barabbas, but when they did, Pilate was forced to follow through and hand Jesus over to be crucified.

In a desperate attempt to absolve himself of any guilt in the whole affair, he washed his hands in a basin of water and said to the crowd, "I am innocent of this man's blood. It is your responsibility!"

Jesus was crucified, and Pilate, according to legend, was called to Rome and executed for his part in the affair.

ON A WING AND A PRAYER

A good friend of mine, Wayne Duncan, loves flying planes. One day he mentioned a dream he'd had that forewarned him of potential loss of life.

"On the night of Friday January 5th, I woke from a dream in which I had been flying an aeroplane over the Oaks area. I had felt myself at the controls with the whole sensation of flight, but there was a fear inside me; a knowing that this flight was going to end badly. I somehow knew this aeroplane was going to have some kind of structural failure, which inevitably would cause it to crash..."

Wayne told me how in the dream he was flying at a low altitude when the aircraft failed, went into a steep right-hand dive towards the ground. He had felt that he was actually in the plane, his heart racing knowing that it was going to hit the ground at high speed. The detail in this dream was quite amazing.

He continued: *"I saw myself standing in front of the aircraft with spinner and propeller nose first into the dirt. The right hand wheel was torn off from the aeroplane and there was a lot of other structural damage."*

After this detailed, yet disturbing dream, Wayne couldn't sleep for the rest of the night. Realising that he'd planned to go flying the very next day, Saturday 6th of January, he couldn't help but wonder whether the dream was meant as a warning for him or for someone else.

As he drove out to the airfield early the following day, he stopped his car and prayed. "Lord, I have foreseen this crash and I believe it could be fatal. I pray for whoever is involved, that a miracle will occur and they will walk away uninjured."

Wayne taxied his plane out of the hanger, proceeded to do a more thorough than usual pre-flight inspection, not once or twice, but three times. Eventually he climbed into his plane and took off from the runway strip, and a little later returned safe and sound.

Soon after, a fellow pilot was also taxiing out toward the runway strip with a passenger in the other seat. They hadn't been long in the air when the unthinkable happened. The bonnet of the plane flew off and the plane went into a steep, hard, right, downward turn. It rapidly lost altitude, plummeting toward the ground. As it went crazily over the road and under power lines it hit a pole which broke the left hand wheel off, tore the tail and elevators off and then caused the plane from a height of about 30 metres to nose dive into the ground.

The pilot and the passenger somehow miraculously hopped out of the plane unharmed. Later, the pilot said he'd looked at his air speed indicator just before the final nose dive and it was reading just over 65 knots, which is about 130 km hour for the impact.

Wayne went on to say how terrifying it was, watching the devastation and graphic detail of his dream unfold before his very eyes.

I wonder what would have been the outcome had Wayne not prayed. There is no question that God will use dreams to warn us of impending danger. My suggestion, if such a dream comes your way, is to pray earnestly. I once titled a message, 'Does It Pay to Pray?' What do you think? "A man without prayer is like a tree without roots." Pope Pius XII (1876-1958)[5]

5. DREAMS CAN BE GOD'S WAY OF KEEPING US FROM PRIDE

I once heard it said, "Pride is like a beard; it just keeps growing." When considering the story of King Nebuchadnezzar, I'd say he was long overdue for a shave. When it comes to pride a person may be totally unaware that they even possess such an attitude. To be told that one is proud often causes a defensive reaction, further reinforcing our subconscious denial of this negative trait. The failure to admit pride in one's waking life may manifest itself in a dream. In King Nebuchadnezzar's case, as his success, riches and fame increased, so too did his pride, like a weed that crept into his life. Perhaps one of pride's greatest crimes is failing to recognise that no man achieves anything great in life without the help of another. For King Nebuchadnezzar, a warning in a dream was not enough to turn him from his conceit.

We read in Daniel 4:5 how, after just having preened his proverbial feathers, the king of Babylon had a dream that frightened the living daylights out of him.

"I had a dream," the king replied. "It made me afraid. As I was lying in my bed, the images and visions that passed through my mind terrified me."

God, in His goodness, was trying to bring to King Nebuchadnezzar's attention the pride in his life.

In the book of Job we see how God will use a nightmare in hope that it may divert the course of a person's life from evil to good.

"For God does speak, now one way, now another, though man may not perceive it. In a dream, in a vision of the night, when deep sleep falls on men as they slumber in their beds, he may speak in their ears and terrify them with warnings, to turn man from wrongdoing and *keep him from pride*, to preserve his soul from the pit, his life from perishing by the sword." Job 33: 14-18

After King Nebuchadnezzar had gone through the process of seeking the interpretation from his advisers and finding they had nothing useful to offer, he realised they were unable to help him. It was then that Daniel, the man of God, came forward and the king told him of the dream.

The story continues in Daniel 4:19 "Then Daniel was greatly perplexed for a time, and his thoughts terrified him. So the King said to Daniel "Do not let the dream or its meaning alarm you."

The dream itself (Daniel 4:10-17) was full of judgement and terror, which only by God's grace fell short of a death sentence. The dream was so frightening that even Daniel was shocked and dismayed. Daniel appealed to the king, "My lord, if only the dream applied to your enemies and its meaning to your adversaries..."

The dream revealed how God intended to humble Nebuchadnezzar, and it came to pass exactly as the dream had foretold. Nebuchadnezzar was driven to madness and went out from his palace and lived among the animals of the field, eating grass as though he was an ox. This insanity lasted for seven years.

"At the end of that time I, Nebuchadnezzar, raised my eyes toward heaven, and my sanity was restored. Then I praised the Most High; I honoured and glorified him who lives forever." Daniel 4:34

Here is the humbled king's conclusion: "Now I, Nebuchadnezzar, praise and exalt and glorify the King of heaven, because everything He does is right and all His ways are just. And those who walk in pride He is able to humble." Daniel 4:37

In Daniel Chapter 4:29 God in His goodness and mercy gives the King twelve months to mend his ways. In frightening the king, God's motivation was to steer his life onto the right path.

I once heard a man say, "It is God's job to exalt a man, and it is man's job to humble himself. Should that man decide to do God's job, God will do man's job."

6. DREAMS CAN BE WHAT GOD USES TO GET OUR ATTENTION WHEN WE ARE NOT LISTENING

THE LIVERPOOL KISS

A young man from our church came to see me about a dream his brother had had. His brother had dreamt he saw Jesus as a stone-like figure standing above an empty grave. It looked like the type of religious statue you might see at a traditional church. As the brother dreamed, the stone-like figure of Christ began to come alive in flesh and blood. To his amazement and stunned surprise Jesus began to move toward him. As the Lord made His approach, the brother was overwhelmed with the love coming from the Lord's eyes, but was suddenly taken back when Jesus came up to him and gave him a 'Liverpool Kiss' (headbutt).

The young man woke up puzzled at what he had just dreamt and shared it with his brother, who felt sure there was something in it.

As we sat talking, the dreamer's brother told me how he had been trying to reach him. He'd told him the difference Jesus had made in his own life, and encouraged him to give his life to Christ as well. The trouble was, the dreamer's impression of Christ was nothing more than some religious ornament, collecting dust in a church sanctuary.

The empty grave in the dream was giving authority to the Bible when it says that on the third day Christ rose from the dead. To the young man, Jesus was no more than a lifeless stone-like piece of religious memorabilia. As the dream unfolded, Jesus took on the very nature of a living and breathing human form, accentuated by the compassion and love that radiated from his being. Jesus made his approach to the young man and gave him a 'Liverpool Kiss'. I had to ask what a 'Liverpool Kiss' was as it wasn't something I was familiar with and sounded intriguing.

It turned out that he loved watching soccer and Liverpool was his favourite club. Apparently, Liverpool players are known to approach their opposing player, just as the whistle blows for the game to begin, and give him a headbutt, an action known as the 'Liverpool Kiss'. This act is to convey the message to the other party that "Hey! You're Mine!"

When I discovered the meaning of the 'Liverpool Kiss', the dream was no longer a mystery to me. Jesus came up to this young man and gave him a 'Liverpool Kiss', as if to say "Hey, I want you to be mine, an action that he could relate to."

When I first heard the dream I couldn't help laughing. Imagine Jesus head-butting a man. Now that is way out and wild. The Lord hasn't changed, has He? He's challenging our religious concept of Him, and loves to reach out to man using whatever method will best relate to the individual.

7. DREAMS CAN REVEAL THE FUTURE

Some dreams have an ability to draw back the curtain from tomorrow for a sneak preview of what's to come. There are times where the Lord may choose to open the window into the future and reveal a snap-shot of His will for your life.

Pharaoh was warned of an approaching famine; Nebuchadnezzar, of the Kingdoms to come; I often dream of preaching in various nations, most of which I have never visited. Concerning my own dreams I have to say that timing and preparation are everything. I have no doubt that I will be there in person one day. But I didn't realise just how soon it would be before that would begin.

DESTINY WITH DENMARK

I woke up from a dream and found myself muttering to myself, over and over like a broken record. "I've got to go to Denmark to preach, I've got

*to go to Denmark to preach. It's important that I go to Denmark. I don't
know anyone in Denmark, except for Mal Fletcher. April is a good time
to go, I need to go in April."*

That morning I phoned the former National leader of my
denomination.

I said to him, "John, you have travelled extensively; what do you
know about Denmark?"

He answered, "What is your interest in Denmark."

I explained the dream and he said, "the National leader of our
churches in Denmark flies into Melbourne in three or four week's
time. I'll arrange an appointment for you to see him."

What I didn't know when I met him, was that prior to leaving his
nation, he and a group of his colleagues prayed that the Lord would
guide his steps and lead him to specific people. One person they did
pray for him to meet was someone who could impact the youth of
their nation.

**To cut a long story short, this Danish leader invited me to come
to his country. When I went, I spoke in their International Apostolic
Bible College to about one hundred students representing twenty-
two nations. It was an awesome privilege, and I was invited the
following year to do a National Youth Conference, followed by some
time in Italy to speak at their Bi-annual Apostolic Euro Ministers'
Conference. Amazing how one door opens to another, and all from
a dream! I wonder what would have happened if I had just said to
myself, "Oh, it's nothing but a fleeting dream."**

One week before Abraham Lincoln's assassination he had a dream.
Ward Hill Lamon, the president's confidant and lifelong friend, told in
his journals of the night Mr. Lincoln had 'his personal Patmos'. Ward
Hill Lamon recorded the words that Lincoln spoke:

THE AMERICAN PRESIDENT ABRAHAM LINCOLN

"About ten days ago, I retired very late. I had been up waiting for important dispatches from the front. I could not have been long in bed when I fell into a slumber, for I was weary.

I soon began to dream. There seemed to be a deathlike stillness about me. Then I heard subdued sobs, as if a number of people were weeping. I thought I left my bed and wandered downstairs. There the silence was broken by the same pitiful sobbing, but the mourners were invisible.

I went from room to room; no living person was in sight, but the same mournful sounds of distress met me as I passed along. It was light in all the rooms; every object was familiar to me, but where were all the people who were grieving as if their hearts would break? I was puzzled and alarmed. What could be the meaning of all this? Determined to find the cause of a state of things so mysterious and so shocking, I kept on until I arrived at the East Room, which I entered. There I met with a sickening surprise.

Before me was a corpse wrapped in funeral vestments. Around it were stationed soldiers who were acting as guards, and there was a throng of people, some gazing mournfully upon the corpse, whose face was covered, others weeping pitifully. "Who is dead in the White House?" I demanded of one of the soldiers. "The president," was his answer; "he was killed by an assassin!" Then came a loud burst of grief from the crowd, which awoke me from my dream, I have been strongly annoyed by it ever since.

'That is horrid,' said Mrs Lincoln. 'I wish you had not told it. I am glad I don't believe in dreams, or I should be in terror from this time forth.'

'Well,' responded Mr. Lincoln thoughtfully, 'it was only a dream, Mary. Let us say no more about it, and try to forget it. I think the Lord in His own good time and way will work this out all right. God knows what is best.'"

The president began to study various passages in the Bible in order to discover something about the importance of the dream. This did not serve to make him any wiser, however, for on the night he was shot, he had chosen to go to the theatre without any bodyguards.

The history of the United States could well have been changed had the president paid more attention to his dream and taken precautionary measures to protect himself. When someone dreams of such an incident, it does not necessarily mean that it will happen. It may well be a warning to be more careful. Perhaps the sorrow of such an event could have been avoided by simply stepping up security.[6]

In this case it could be said, a dream was revealing the future so that a needless tragedy might have been avoided. But not all dreams speak literally of the future. One needs to be careful about jumping to such conclusions.

Many of us have on occasion awoken from an upsetting or distressing dream. Often, our natural reaction is to believe the dream or take it as literal. As a safeguard I would recommend we pray a prayer of divine protection and covering for the subjects of the dream, and remember there is every chance the dream is of a metaphorical nature.

I know of a person who dreamt that his father died, and he woke up with tears trickling down his face. His most immediate reaction was to call his dad and see that he was all right. Over the years he had many dreams where his father died, but on this occasion it was the most disturbing of them all. It turned out to be the last time he would dream such a thing. The numerous dreams of his father's death were messages in which the dream was telling the dreamer that there were certain attributes and characteristics that he possessed from his father that were no longer going to be part of his life.

We will look at the area of people and death in dreams later in the book.

Not every dream is foretelling the future and therefore, careful consideration needs to be given to its possible symbolic meaning. Should you dream of a car speeding, the driver losing control and slamming into a brick wall, it may be that the pace of your life is out of hand and you are beginning to lose control. Perhaps you dream someone has stabbed you in the back, but it doesn't necessarily mean that you remain indoors and refrain from public life; rather it could be an indicator that someone has been 'back-stabbing you at work'.

CHAPTER 4

Why are dreams hard to understand?

"Dreams are a subjective landscape in which mountains and molehills are easily confused. Making sense of them is more an art than a science."

Ann Spangler

While some dreams can be easily understood, most are loaded with symbols of all kinds. In our western way of life we are primarily taught to think logically and verbally, and not symbolically.

Ann Spangler, in her book *Dreams: Miracles Can Happen in the Middle of the Night*, illustrates the conflict associated with interpreting your dreams.

"Dreams are a subjective landscape in which mountains and molehills are easily confused. Making sense of them is more an art than a science."[1]

Herman Riffel refers to the language of the dream and describes it as being different from the language of the mind.

"Dreams are the language of the heart. The mind speaks in the language of thoughts and concepts, while dreams speak in the language of pictures and symbols."[2]

Unlike eastern culture, our western way of thinking is given more to rationalism and logic, rather than symbols and pictures.

QUESTION ONE:
IS IT WRONG TO INTERPRET DREAMS?

Some Christian people are apprehensive at even thinking of interpreting dreams.

I came across a well-meaning lady who was convinced my teaching was not biblical and concerned that what I was encouraging was wrong. In a meeting with her and her pastor I listened carefully to her objections. I could tell she was agitated about the whole thing and so I took the time to assure her that she should feel free to talk and even told her that her thoughts might prove to be helpful to me. After all, I am a man on a journey, accountable to those over me and open to hearing other opinions. I have long since learnt that one can learn something from almost anyone.

One of her main concerns was that what I was teaching was not biblical. She maintained that if God gives a dream to someone it doesn't need interpreting; that He will speak to the person so that it can be clearly understood.

My answer to this is yes and no. Yes, there are many occasions when God makes a dream clear and simple enough to understand. The answer is also no, it is not always as simple as that. The Bible gives us references to back up this statement.

We see in Genesis that God gave Pharaoh a dream, which he did not understand even though God gave it to him. The meaning of the dream was not clear.

"The reason the dream was given to Pharaoh in two forms is that the matter has been firmly decided by God, and God will do it soon." Genesis 41:32. Pharaoh needed Joseph to interpret the dream.

We see also in Daniel chapter 4 that King Nebuchadnezzar had a dream. In verse 18 he asks Daniel to tell him what it means. Here is another case where God gave the king a dream and the dreamer has difficulty understanding it. King Nebuchadnezzar needed Daniel to interpret it for him. In verse 19 Daniel makes an admission that he is perplexed by the dream's symbolism and ponders over it for a time. Here again we have a case where the dream is not immediately clear, even to Daniel.

We see in the book of Mark chapter 4 where Jesus uses certain symbols to illustrate his point in the parable of the 'Sower and the Seed'.

One would have thought that by this time, after having spent so much time listening to Jesus teaching, the disciples would quickly and easily understand the Lord's parables. But apparently they didn't understand. Verse 13, Jesus turns to them and says, "...Don't you understand this parable? How then will you understand any parable?" and proceeds to explain the symbols within the parable.

Another Scripture this time in Job 33:14-15 reminds us God is constantly speaking to people though they are not recognizing it. "For God does speak - now one way, now another - though man may not perceive it. In a dream, in a vision of the night when deep sleep falls on men..."

QUESTION TWO:
WHY DOES GOD SOMETIMES SPEAK IN RIDDLES?

Numbers 12:6 sheds some light on the matter. "When a prophet of the Lord is among you, I reveal myself to him in visions, I speak to him in dreams. But this is not true of my servant Moses; he is faithful in all my house. With him I speak face to face, *clearly* and not in *riddles...*"

Why would God conceal things in riddles, parables and dreams? Perhaps the Heavenly Father, like some of us, just wants to play *Hide and Seek* with His children. The Scriptures are welcoming us to seek Him out.

"So I say to you: *Ask* and it will be given to you; *seek* and you will find; knock and the door will be opened to you." Luke 11:9

"It is the glory of God to conceal a matter; to search out a matter is the glory of kings." Proverbs 25:2

"The kingdom of heaven is like treasure hidden in the field. When a man found it..." Matthew 13:44

QUESTION THREE:
IS IT WRONG TO EXPLORE SYMBOLS?

Another objection raised in that meeting was that we shouldn't be encouraging a *dream code.*

I knew what she was talking about; I cover this area a little later in 'Your personal dictionary of symbols'. She questioned why I would want to look into what a bird might mean, or transport, or trees, or water etc. She thought it a futile and foolish exercise that was not biblically validated.

By now I felt a little as if I was before *Judge Judy* awaiting sentencing. Yet I knew how important these questions were to someone who was earnest and sincere in their desire to stand for truth.

I assured the lady that I was not trying to encourage a so-called 'code'. Rather my aim was to bring people to an understanding that the Bible, like our dreams, is full of symbolism. We in western culture are very linear in our thinking and, unlike other cultures, are less likely to think metaphorically and symbolically.

If I were to ask what passages of Scripture use the symbol of *water,* and what do they represent, a common answer would be:

Psalm 23:2 "...He leads me beside quiet waters..."

Another passage easily remembered is from Matthew chapter 7, where Jesus uses a parable to illustrate his message, and in it uses the symbol of water to portray turbulent, troublesome, and trying times. As you read this passage you will note its rich use of symbolism.

Matthew 7:24-28 "Therefore everyone who hears these words of mine and puts them into practice is like a wise man who built his *house* on a *rock*. The *rain* came down, the *streams rose*, and the *winds blew* and beat against that house; yet it did *not fall*, because it had its *foundation* on the rock. But everyone who hears these words of mine and does not put them into practice is like a foolish man who built his house on *sand*. The rain came down and the streams rose, and the winds blew and beat against that house, and it fell with a *great crash*. When Jesus had finished saying these things, the crowds were amazed at His teaching..."

Unlike the calm and stillness of Psalm 23 the water in Matthew 7 is agitated and stormy. So it is with life; there are times where our days are running smoothly and quietly and other days they can be stormy, agitated and choppy. To me, water in this instance can be a symbol of life's circumstances. When one dreams we could ask the question: is the water murky, clear, still, choppy and agitated? Are you swimming with the current or against the flow? Perhaps you are treading water. Is there a large wave approaching and you find yourself saying, "I have to get over this?" Water may also mean different things to different people; water took on the symbol of the grave at the Jordan River in which Jesus was baptised. Many of us are familiar with the movie, *The Ten Commandments,* where the waters open up for the nation of Israel to pass through the Red Sea.

In the same passage Jesus refers to the *house* as a symbol of one's life. He refers to *sand* and *rock*, symbolic for foundations, *waves* and the *wind* as the trials of life. This passage makes it abundantly clear, whether a person is a Christian or not, both parties are exposed to the elements of pressure and pain in life. The question is what type of house is it, where is it, and what is it built on? Who is in the house, what is in it that should not be, and so on. We will look at the symbol of a house a little further on in the book.

It is interesting to note that studies have showed that 40% of our dreams consist of houses.

Another example is the metaphor of a tree. The Bible uses the tree as a symbol in several passages of scripture. Can you think of when the tree is used and in what context?

In almost every case I have found the tree, like the house, to be a metaphor of one's life. Notice in the following passages: where the tree is planted; the condition and health of the tree; its size; the type of tree it is; what type of life exists in the tree; the types of fruit it yields etc.

A tree planted by a stream

"He is like a tree planted by streams of water, which yields its fruit in season and whose leaf does not whither..." Psalm1:3

A tree as high as the sky

"These are the visions I saw while lying in my bed: I looked, and there before me stood a tree in the middle of the land. Its height was enormous. The tree grew large and strong and its top touched the sky; it was visible to the ends of the earth. Its leaves were beautiful. Its fruit abundant, and on it was food for all. Under it the beasts of the field found shelter, and the birds of the air lived in its branches; from it every creature was fed."

What do you suppose these images are speaking about?

WHAT HAPPENS TO THIS GLORIOUS TREE?

"In the visions I saw while lying on my bed, I looked, and there before me was a messenger, a Holy one, coming down from heaven. He called in a loud voice: 'Cut down the tree and trim off its branches; strip off its leaves and scatter its fruit; let the animals flee from under it and the birds from its branches. But let the stump and its roots, bound with iron and bronze, remain in the ground, in the grass of the field."

This picture of a tree was one of King Nebuchadnezzar's dreams and is recorded in Daniel 4: 9-15. Sadly Daniel had to tell the king the dream was talking about his life and empire. Daniel gives the full interpretation in verse 19.

Once again the symbol of a tree may mean something entirely different to someone else. It could represent the family tree as is mentioned later in the book. Perhaps for someone who works in a forest as a ranger, a tree could hold an entirely different meaning. The interpretation must always be left to the dreamer to witness to its truth and never assume that one symbol means the same for everyone.

With over seven hundred accounts of dreams and visions in the Bible there is much we can learn from its rich symbolism in parables, dreams and visions.

By the end of the interview with this lady, I was not certain whether I had been able to satisfy all her questions and the objections that she raised, but it did serve to motivate me to dig further into the Bible to confirm my convictions, and help me to know that I was on the right track.

THE UNLIMITED LANGUAGE OF PARABLES

The saying 'a picture paints a thousand words' is so true. The same could be said of a dream. One picture, one symbol has the ability to open up the meaning of an entire dream.

An Arabian Proverb has this to say: "He who is the best preacher turns an ear into an eye."

Jesus knew the power behind the use of symbols in a parable. He was a master at it, and there was no one quite like Him. He possessed the ability and divine inspiration to paint verbally some of the finest masterpieces showing Christian living by using imagery and symbolism. Herman Riffel puts it like this:

"Jesus commonly spoke in parables. He told wonderful stories out of every day life, which the people could understand. When Jesus spoke of the yeast of the Pharisees, the disciples at first took Him literally, but he explained that He was speaking symbolically. He spoke of Himself as a door, a vine, and a shepherd, as bread and as wine. He did not use the language of reason in describing himself, *for this kind of language is far too limited. Symbolic language is infinite.*"[3]

The following is a list of the Lord's parables; one can learn much from the symbolism contained in them.[4]

* * * * * *

PARABLE	MATTHEW	MARK	LUKE
Lamp under a bowl	5:14-15	4:21-22	8:16; 11:33
The two builders	7:24-27	6:47-49	
New & old cloth	9:16	2:21	5:36
The wine skins	9:17	2:22	5:37-38
Sower & the soils	13:3-8, 18-23	4:3-8, 14-20	8:5-8, 11-15
Wheat & the weeds	13:24-30,36-43		
The mustard seed	13:31-32	4:30-32	13:18-19
The Yeast	13:33		13:20-21
Hidden Treasure	13:44		
Valuable Pearl	13:45-46		
The net	13:47-50		
Owner of a house	13:52		
Lost sheep	18:12-14		15:4-7
Unmerciful servant	18:23-34		
The Vineyard	20:1-16		
The two sons	21:28-32		
The tenants	21:33-44	12:1-11	20:9-18
Wedding banquet	22:2-14		
Fig Tree	24:32-35	13:28-29	21:29-31
Wise servant	24:45-51		12:42-48
Ten virgins	25:1-13		
The talents	25:14-30		19:12-27
Sheep & goats	25:31-46		
The growing seed		4:26-29	
Watchful servants		13:35-37	12:35-40
Money lender			7:41-43
Good Samaritan			10:30-37
Friend in need			11:5-8

CHAPTER 5

Understanding the dreams you dream

"Treating dreams like junk mail, we often throw away the very answers we ask for when we pray for counsel or guidance."[1]

Ira Milligan

SYMBOLS - THE LANGUAGE OF DREAMS

There is no end to the list of symbols in dreams. They can be just about anything: a house, an ocean, people, a car, a ship, a tree, an airport, death, babies. You could find yourself climbing a mountain that might indicate a possible promotion or lift in life; perhaps even a sense of gaining new heights. It may suggest that you are making a mountain out of a molehill and that you are over amplifying a problem.

Alternatively you might dream about being in a valley. Perhaps you're going through a low spot, struggling with low self-esteem.

In Psalm 23:4 the valley is described as a place of death and despair and the believer is reassured the Lord is with them and they ought not fear any evil while they are going through it.

Books have been written and seminars conducted using various symbols to describe personalities; for example, volcanoes for people with eruptive natures; snipers - those who like taking critical shots at people; bulldozers - people with a know-it-all attitude who care little for the opinions of others.

Symbols have long been part of the language of poets, moviemakers, artists and songwriters and they are also the universal language for dreams.

Whatever colour, creed, race or tongue, we can all communicate far easier with each other with pictures rather than words.

ONE WORD (SYMBOL) AT A TIME

Understanding the language of symbols is not as easy as one might think. That it is why, like Daniel and Joseph, we ought to seek the Lord for revelation and insight. It is important to note that the way to understand symbols is like the way we often learn the English language – one word at a time, that is, one or two symbols at a time.

I remember when our family first moved to Australia, and the emotional torment I felt at six years of age, having to learn a foreign language. I would come home from school distressed and crying, hoping that mum would be able to help me. She would be equally frustrated knowing no more than I did. As time went by, one word or phrase at a time, one day at a time, I began to master one of the most difficult languages in the world. I was born in former Yugoslavia, and the language spoken there, like most European languages, is phonetic—in other words, you spell the word the way it sounds. Not so with the English language, and to this day I struggle to see why we have silent letters, double letters, two letters to make the one sound, letters where there shouldn't be letters and letters where there should be other letters.

Lets face it, English is a strange language: there is no egg in eggplant, no ham in hamburger and no pine in the pineapple. We sometimes take English for granted but if we examine its paradoxes we find that quicksand takes you down slowly, boxing rings are square and if the plural of tooth is teeth, shouldn't the plural of phone booth be phone beeth. Anyway I'm sure we get the general (also a military rank) idea.

Two senior students were appointed to help me conquer what seemed like the Mount Everest of all languages. With very little progress at first, one of them came up with an idea. Instead of trying to have me repeat the word, they would point to the picture and say, "Now repeat after me." So it was, that I discovered my first English words, d-o-g and c-a-t. I quickly learnt by associating the picture with the word.

Often in a seminar setting I do a similar exercise only in reverse fashion. I ask the audience to think of a picture that best describes the word.

For instance, when I ask the people to paint me a picture that best describes the word 'calm', invariably 90% of the crowd say still water, or calm sea. Alternatively, if I said the word 'storm' many would suggest turbulent waters and high waves. If I ask for a description of the word 'success' the reply is often, ladder. Another person might describe success with a picture of a mountaintop, and others say that when they think of success they think of a tall building.

Symbols like these will often appear in our dreams, at which time you could ask yourself what the image represents to you.

I asked an audience what image they would use to illustrate stability. Some said a strong tree; others mentioned a foundation to a building, or a rock.

During a time of intense trial, I had a dream where I found myself on top of a rock some ten metres out into the shallows. Looking back at the ocean I felt overcome with panic as I saw enormous waves approaching. They were at least one hundred feet high, larger than anything I had seen before. Perhaps the only time I have seen anything that was close to this was in the movie 'Perfect Storm', in which a fishing trawler fails to make it over an insurmountable wave.

With the same degree of anxiety and panic that the fisherman displayed in the movie, clutching firmly onto the rock I waited for the inevitable. In no time at all the distant roar of the huge swell was upon me. Like the folding of an envelope, the force of the first wave tried to swallow me up. Still holding on, the second wave was equally merciless. I was wondering when this was going to end, yet wave after wave spun me like a bottle top. Eventually the ocean roar subsided to a calm. Once the danger had passed I slid down from the rock unscathed, climbed up a small embankment and made my way up to the top where the road was.

Perhaps you can see how appropriate the symbols in this dream were in relation to the trials I was going through. The rock was symbolic of Jesus Christ in whom I had put my trust and faith during this intense and difficult time. Jesus used various symbols to refer to himself. He spoke of himself as a door, as bread, light, a vine and a rock. In my dream He was a rock. Psalm 18:2 "The Lord is my *rock*, my fortress and my deliverer."

The amazing thing about this rock was that in my dream it was some twenty feet higher than the pounding waves. I have always found that my faith in Christ is able to match whatever is thrown at me. Isaiah 59:19, "When the enemy (trials, difficulties and onslaught of evil) comes in like a flood, the spirit of the Lord will raise up a standard against him." (KJV)

YOUR PERSONAL DICTIONARY OF SYMBOLS

I encourage you to begin writing your own journal and recording your dreams; start to build your own personal vocabulary of symbols. Each person's dreams are unique to themselves as are their symbols.

Dream books or dream dictionaries in which you can look up

the meanings of dream themes and symbols may prove helpful, but can also prove useless. One person may dream of eating chillies, and to that person it may mean things are a little hot; to you however, it might mean things are a little cold.

A hawk may represent your pet bird, while to another person it might portray his football team, and to yet another it might represent a bird of prey, circling ready for its chance to attack. A dream dictionary might suggest the dreamer should keep a 'hawk's eye' on someone or some situation, another might tell you that the ancient symbol for a hawk is intelligence or good luck.

You cannot define a symbol and have it mean the same thing for every single person. This is where we need the guidance and insight of the Holy Spirit. John 16:13 tells us, "But when he, the Spirit of truth, comes, he will guide you into all truth…"

May I recommend Ira Milligan's book *Understanding the Dreams You Dream*, as a tremendous resource of scriptural symbols. Morton T Kelsey recommends Ad de Vries's *Dictionary of Symbols and Imagery* as one of the most sophisticated and helpful resources of the many meanings conveyed by symbols.

ONE SYMBOL CAN HOLD MULTIPLE MEANINGS

One symbol may have multiple meanings just as one word can.

Consider these words and what they mean:

Break: To destroy; take time out; interrupt; broken down etc.

Foul: dirty; or when something is out of bounds; it is also a sporting term commonly used in baseball and boxing.

Palm: The flat part of your up-turned hand or a tree; or to *palm off* something onto someone else. For a rower it can mean the blade of an oar, for others an instrument for sewing canvas.

One symbol can mean different things to different people, often depending on context.

To one person a *lion* may mean 'The Lion of the tribe of Judah', a reference to Jesus, Revelation 5:5. To another it could symbolise evil, "...the devil prowls around like a roaring lion..." 1 Peter 5:8. Yet again it could be referring to a Christian: "... but the righteous are as bold as a lion." Proverbs 28:1.

Take the *snake* as another example: For one person it can be a symbol for evil: "Now the serpent was more crafty than any of the wild animals..." Genesis 3:1. Depending on the context of the dream the serpent could stand for the power of God. In Exodus 7:9 Moses' staff is thrown to the ground and turns into a snake. Pharaoh's sorcerers and magicians threw their staffs down and each became a snake. Moses' snake (staff) displayed its superior power and authority by eating the others. Then again a snake may symbolise the life of a Christian: "Therefore be as shrewd as snakes and as innocent as doves." Matthew 10:16. Whatever the case, each symbol should be looked at in its context to the dream and the dreamer.

MY VOCABULARY OF DREAMS

The following descriptions of symbols come from my personal experiences and research, both with my own dreams and through helping others to interpret their dreams. I share these thoughts to serve only as helpful suggestions. The true meaning of any symbol must always remain with the dreamer to work through.

HOUSE

As I've mentioned before, it's been said that 40% of our dreams are made up of houses. Personally, I've usually found the house to represent my life. Is it old or new? Is it run down or in good condition, small or large? Where are you in the house? Are you in the attic? Is it dark inside?

Perhaps you've dreamed you're in the basement, kitchen, or study. The bedroom can be seen as the place of intimacy or the place of rest. The toilet with its normal function may indicate something you need to dispose of. It may be the house you were raised in as a child, indicating something to do with your past or upbringing. It could be two storeys; the second floor could refer to your spiritual life. Is someone or something trying to break into your home? Have you woken up in your work clothes? Your work life could be interfering with your relationship at home. The size of the home may hold meaning. Remember my dream when the visitors asked how many squares my house was. The location of the home may have significance, and also the décor. Perhaps, like the three little pigs, what it's made of may hold an important key.

CLOTHES

Do you find yourself coming home in your work clothes? It could be, as I found out in my own life, symbolising that your work life is interfering with your home life. Sometimes people find themselves at work with their pyjamas on. This could mean that an aspect of your domestic life is clashing with your work life. But then, on the other hand, perhaps you're a workaholic who has need of rest; then again, maybe you are sleeping on the job.

When you notice specifically what you are wearing in a dream, you have to ask what that might mean. For instance, suppose you dream of wearing an expensive gown. Could it mean that perhaps you are of much greater value than you give yourself credit for?

Old clothes may reflect a need for creativity and change. Similarly, outgrown clothes can be symbolic of growing up and maturing. Washing your clothes could illustrate a need to clean up certain attitudes or areas in your life. Are the clothes you're wearing your own or do they belong to someone else? If so, who is that person and what do they remind you of?

GOAL FOR IT

I remember dreaming I was playing soccer in my work shoes. I was having the time of my life kicking one goal after another. There was nothing the keeper could do to stop me.

To me it seemed obvious that I was approaching a time in my life where many of my unfulfilled goals would soon be achieved. In this dream the shoes were the key; I was playing with my *work* shoes. Not long after that I was in Perth on a ministry trip. One morning I went for a walk without paying close attention to where I was going. Eventually I found myself in the centre of a football oval, and I sensed a word from the Holy Spirit: "The ball is about to bounce and the siren soon to sound." I had a great sense both through the dream and the prophetic word that I was going to score some major goals.

A PERFECT AND PLEASANT FIT

I was twenty-two years of age when I went to work full time as a minister. Feeling very inadequate for the task ahead, I had this dream:

I found myself entering a delicatessen or milk bar. I thought this worth noting as years earlier I'd dreamt I was in a 747 jumbo jet that I thought was going to take off but instead taxied me to a small milk bar and stopped. However this time I dreamed I was entering another milk bar. It was located in a very classy area. As I walked in, I noticed it was not quite the same as it used to be (I believe this was referring to my previous dream with the plane). It was no longer a milk bar but rather it looked more like a department store. The store was very spacious and nicely presented, and contained various items of merchandise from jewellery to clothing. I made my way to the clothing department and it all looked to be secondhand. (I felt this reflected my feeling of inadequacy). *However, I came across a brand new blue suit. I went to the change rooms and took off my old clothes to put on this new outfit. It was very comfortable* (indicating that the ministry was going to sit right with me). *Then I turned around and saw a plate of lollies and when I tried one I found it to be sweet and delicious* (the ministry was not going to be a sour experience).

In this case, it was clear to me that the Holy Spirit was using the dream to tell me that I was 'suited' to the task and not to worry.

What you are wearing can give important clues to the actual meaning of a dream. It is important to note that if you dream of walking around with nothing on, this, too, is very significant. Please refer to the section on nudity.

TRANSPORTATION

I often dream I'm at the airport when suddenly I realise I have left my passport at home. Such a dream is a reflection of what is going on in my real life. I travel on planes a lot and my worst fear is that I will arrive at the airport and will have forgotten my passport.

Dreaming of travel may relate to an upcoming trip, but then again it could be a metaphor for your journey in life. Give attention to the details about your trip. Where are you going? Are you travelling with someone else? If so, with whom? Do you have luggage with you? What is happening along the way?

CAR

I remember a dream in earlier years where my father had given me the keys to a brand new model Mercedes Benz. It was gold in colour and full of luxurious accessories. As I drove off with the whole family inside, I barely managed to keep it on the road. Two-motorcycle policemen were approaching fast behind me. They pulled me over and had a word or two to say about my driving, then left and signalled me to keep going. I was surprised they didn't book me.

I believed the car resembled my personal potential and that God our Heavenly Father gave me a picture of the importance of the call and gifting on my life that took the form of a gold Mercedes Benz. I began to drive recklessly but the divine authority, instead of taking the vehicle away, seemed to give me, the inexperienced driver, time to master the calling and gifting.

A car might represent your personal life and direction you are travelling. Again you have to ask yourself a number of questions: what type of car is it? Is it a jeep, which might indicate a rugged journey ahead? Perhaps you've dreamed of an eight-seater van, a people mover, which could mean you are going somewhere, and guiding or leading a number of people along the same path. Is it a big or small car? How fast is the car travelling, too fast or too slow? Has it gone off the main road or taken a wrong turn? Where are you going and is there a purpose for going there? The needle of the tachometer may be past the red line, which may imply, as with a vehicle, that you are pushing yourself too hard with a life style of excessive stress. Smoke may be coming from under the bonnet or the car could have a flat tyre, indicating fatigue. Perhaps you have a puncture that may indicate a burst bubble of your idea or dream.

I remember hearing of a dream from a pastor who'd dreamt he had a flat tyre. In his case I felt the dream was talking about his pastoral team. He had four staff pastors and one of them was not travelling well and needed attention.

The car could have reached a dead end street or been part of an accident. There are numerous examples and the Holy Spirit could use any one of these situations to speak to you in a dream.

PLANE

Sometimes I've seen the planes in my dreams as vehicles of ministry. Dreaming of a large passenger plane may represent working in a large organisation or church denomination. A small plane might indicate a small personal ministry opportunity. Some planes never seem to get off the ground, and there have been occasions when I've found myself taxiing the whole way from one city to the next. In some dreams you may start off, but can't maintain altitude and come back down again, but are nowhere near the airport or launching place, and end up travelling along roads and streets, ducking trees and power lines.

In the years when I had just begun working as a minister, I would often dream of a Boeing 747. I remember the dream where we were ready for take off and all it did was taxi through the city and stop at a milk bar. I believe the Lord was using the plane as a reflection of my life. It became symbolic of my calling or gifting that had the capacity to go far and travel high in life. However, I was not ready for those sorts of altitudes and this implied a lack of preparation.

I like Jim Rohn's comment: "If you want more in life you need to become more."

The fact that the jumbo jet stopped at a milk bar in my dream was something that I noted with interest. "You need milk not solid food..." Hebrews 5:12. When I considered that the Bible encourages us to grow from feeding only on milk, to gradually include manna and then meat, I felt it was clear that a lot more work was needed in my own life before I would be able to soar to new heights.

Attitude always precedes altitude.

When considering a symbol like a plane, again we should ask ourselves questions. What type of plane is it and what is it doing?

The plane could be flying around in circles and getting nowhere, or it could be on the ground, in the air or travelling to a particular place. A wrecked plane might imply a company's collapse or broken dreams.

CRASH LANDING

I dreamt I was flying to Taiwan. Along the way the plane was diving, and it looked as though it was going to crash. I felt unsettled yet didn't panic.

A healing evangelist had invited me to jointly minister with him in Taiwan. I accepted the invitation with a sense of apprehension. I had never done anything like that before or been involved in that type of ministry.

I felt the dream was highlighting my insecurity by showing the plane plummeting toward earth. The feeling tone of the dream was important: I didn't panic; it was rather an unsettling feeling, insecurity.

BOAT

A boat is another mode of transportation. Like the plane and the car this too can represent your life. The boat may be large or small. It could be a speedboat telling you that you are going too fast. It could be travelling through choppy waters, indicating turbulent times of life. It might be a large vessel tied at the docks, perhaps suggesting that it's time to untie those restrictions in your life and set sail. When considering such a dream, it is interesting to note what engineers tell us about a ship tied to the wharf; that it will rust out and wear out faster than if it is out at sea. This is a powerful thought. People who lack vision and direction in their life come to ruin quicker than those willing to have a go in life.

Is the boat drifting, implying a lack of direction? Perhaps it is sinking. You may be carrying the weight of the world on your shoulders and need to throw unnecessary baggage overboard. Is the ship leaking, reflecting depression and stress and a need to cry out for help?

There are many more analogies. The interpretation always lies with the dreamer.

Other symbols for transport may include a train, truck, furniture removalist, helicopter, motorbike, pushbike etc:

TRANSITION

Now this is an area that affects us all. Each of us finds ourselves moving from one experience to another. It could be a change in career, church, location, school or friends. The Bible sums up transition wonderfully when it talks of going from the old to the new. 2 Corinthians 5:17 and Isaiah 43:18-19.

Transition is often a place of frustration; a place of waiting just prior to the birth of something new in your life. It is what stands between the old as it brings in the new. We saw an example of this earlier when I dreamed of a doctor's waiting room.

THE ACOUSTIC AND ELECTRIC GUITAR

Once I had a dream where I found myself standing before a church congregation playing an acoustic guitar. Then someone came and gave me an electric guitar to play and I had both guitars strapped around my neck. I felt rather ridiculous walking around with two guitars around my neck. I knew I wanted to play the electric guitar but before I could, I had to take off the old acoustic guitar.

When considering this dream, I came to the conclusion that the Holy Spirit was showing me that I was coming into a season of change, a time that would bring with it a greater 'amplification' or greater effectiveness (the electric guitar). However, as the dream clearly showed, in order to touch this new level of effectiveness I would have to take off the old (the acoustic guitar). I had to ponder and pray more over the dream, as I hadn't quite understood what the acoustic guitar was representing, but in asking the Holy Spirit for further insight the following revelation came:

The acoustic guitar is a hollow instrument and can produce only one sound. The electric guitar is a solid instrument with the ability to produce multiple sounds. Because it operates on electricity it can be amplified and carry the sound further than the acoustic.

In my dream, both instruments' strings were tuned. This I felt was an important detail. If they had been out of tune I would have questioned whether there might have been a few things in my character that needed looking at.

NEW BOOK, NEW LOOK

I dreamt I was at a large church waiting to preach. I sat in the front row with both my old and new Bibles, flicking through the pages, looking for the text I was to preach on. I noticed it was 6:57pm, and we were approaching that part of the service where I would be invited to preach. At the right moment, I made my way up to the platform taking with me my new Bible, leaving the old one behind.

The dream occurred during a time when I was about to take on itinerant preaching, accepting invitations from different churches to speak. I had already set a date when I would become itinerant rather than just pastor at one location. When I considered this date, the 1st of July, I recalled the time on the clock in my dream. It had been 6:57 pm. To me the time represented the sixth month soon to turn over into the seventh. I believe the dream was also showing me that I was coming into a new expression and revelation of the Scriptures. This was reflected in the transition from the old Bible to my new one.

Transition can also be represented in dreams of a change in clothing, or a change in shoes or shoe size. Perhaps you might find yourself in the transit lounge at the airport. Really it could be anything: a change of brief case might mean a change in employment. Once I changed offices in a dream. In any instance, the theme will revolve around a change of some sort or another.

WISDOM

I received a distressed letter from a young man. He had arrived back at his apartment earlier than expected and walked into his apartment only to find his roommate and a young woman both hurriedly dressing. Somehow word of the unfortunate incident got back to the church pastor, who in turn asked this young man about what he had witnessed. He covered for his roommate by twisting the facts, but later that night he had the following dream:

WISDOM TOOTH

The dream consisted of several scenes. In one scene he found himself pulling a wisdom tooth out and throwing it to the ground.

The dream troubled him greatly, and as it had only been a short time since he'd been to one of my seminars on dreams, he decided to write to me. My immediate response to him was that the tooth (wisdom) being pulled out and thrown to the ground represented a foolish move on his behalf to conceal truth. I went on to encourage him to talk to his friend and make sure that the matter was brought into the open so that it could be dealt with properly.

The symbol of wisdom will appear to the dreamer in a way that relates to the individual. It could be your grandfather whom you've looked to for counsel in everyday life, or a respected teacher. Wisdom can even choose to come in the form of a judge or authority figure.

COLOURS

I dreamt that I was driving a *gold* Mercedes Benz and to me gold represented something of value and importance.

When I was feeling inadequate about becoming a minister, I had the dream where I was in a department store where the goods seemed to be second hand. Though I was feeling a little second hand I put on a *blue* suit. Whenever I think of the colour blue, I think of the sky and the saying, "The sky's the limit." I also think of 'the deep blue sea.' In that context I felt my dream was telling me that the type of ministry God was calling me to would have great height to it (achievements) and great depth (substance and character).

SHIFTING OFFICES

As we have seen, the symbol for transition can come in different forms. I dreamt I was at church, changing offices. Part of the office looked the same, though most of it was different. I was frustrated trying to plug the phone in (the feeling tone is important). I noticed the receiver was pink and I thought it a strange colour for a phone. Our church administrator came in and helped me connect the phone. The telephone system looked a little complex; it seemed to have an international exchange to it.

This dream came at a time when I was due to start in my new role as an itinerant travelling minister. This meant changing a few things: restructuring my time, a change in income and working out a new administrative structure. The international exchange on the phone system that I saw, I believe was a way of saying that God would have me ministering in different nations of the world. I've always understood *pink* to be a relaxing colour, and to me it was an encouragement to be patient and not anxious.

Colours may also be indicative of our emotions and give insight to our moods.

The colour *red* is often associated with different emotions including passion, rage, embarrassment, and at times promiscuous sensual behaviour. Then in complete contrast, red could represent the blood of Jesus Christ in covering our sin.

In both waking and dream life, *red* can suggest warmth, strong emotion or even spontaneous feelings of various sorts. On the other hand, depending on the context of the dream, it could stand for stop, as in the traffic light. *Red* might also mean that you're in the red, taking its meaning from a common saying that means in 'debt'.

Green for me would represent go! In other words, it's all right; I've got the green light. *Green* in a natural sense is the colour of vegetation, forests, lush pastures and full crops. Biblically speaking, Psalm 23 talks about the Lord leading us in green pastures, speaking of peace and provision.

Or it could simply mean growth, as for a healthy green plant. Then there is the saying, 'you're green with envy' and this is another aspect of the colour green, which might hold significance for you.

Yellow is the colour of the sun, the source of warmth, and one of the basic things that sustains life on earth. But then again, yellow is the colour of jaundice, and this is indicative of something quite toxic in the blood.

Purple is often associated with royalty. Lydia in the Bible was the seller of fine purple linen, which was expensive and highly sought after. On the other hand, you could be sporting a purple bruise!

Black is the colour very often associated with evil, darkness of spirit and black magic. Generally, it represents something very dark and oppressive. There may be the odd occasion when something is as black as fine velvet, against which the beauty of jewellery or the stars in the sky may shine.

White usually indicates purity and cleanliness.

There are so many colours that can mean so many things. The clue to the colour rests with the dreamer.

PEOPLE

When you dream about a person, what is it about him or her that is a reflection of your own life. Who are they? And what do they represent to you? What personality traits do they have? Are they dogmatic? Perhaps *you've* been arrogant and inflexible and there may be a need for a flexible, more mature approach in your life. The person you've dreamt about may be intelligent, gentle, fun loving, a leader, decisive. Conversely, there may be a negative trait that you recognise, such as laziness or an inability to make decisions and a lack of conviction. Perhaps seeing these negative characteristics highlights something in your own life that may need attention. You could ask yourself what part of their faultfinding nature and critical spirit has tarnished your character.

A certain minister, who was caught up in an emotional outburst with his son, later had a dream that challenged him greatly. In the dream he shot his mother. His mother represented the gentle side of his life, and it showed him how he had lost his gentle response and control in the dispute with his son.

You may remember the dream in which my wife was watching the television ignoring me. Kate represented the sensitive and intimate side of my marriage. It wasn't that she was ignoring me, rather that I was neglecting her.

Benny Thomas, in his book *Exploring the World Of Dreams,* shares some great insights into this area. He says, "Your friends, family, and co-workers frequently show up in dreams. God can use people to communicate a variety of things in dreams. Among other things they can represent:

THEIR POSITION: Banker, Accountant, Policeman, Pastor etc.
THEIR ATTRIBUTES: Lazy person, smart, rich, poor, organised etc.
THEIR NAME: Names have meanings. Do you know what your
    name means?
THEIR AGE: Mature, childish etc.
THEMSELVES: You dream about Aunt Sarah and the dream really
    does apply to Aunt Sarah. Be cautious here."[2]

HAND IN HAND

Once my wife woke up from a dream in which she found herself walking along holding the hand of a fourteen-year-old. The lad she dreamed of goes to our church and is well known for his devotion to the Lord. The young man's devotion to the Lord was reflected as a symbol of my wife's desire to be close to the Lord.

FREE THE THREE

Several years ago I dreamt I was under the car hiding, and then I found myself in a large room. It seemed like a prison even though it looked like a home, and I couldn't work out why I was locked up for something I did not do. Right here the feeling tone of the dream was really important. I was troubled and bewildered and I kept asking myself why I was locked up for something I did not do?

Overwhelmed with this feeling of no escape, I noticed three chairs. I noted particularly who was sitting on the chairs, and what they were doing. On one of the chairs, which appeared to be a transit lounge seat, sat one of Australia's foremost singing talents. His arms were folded and he was speechless, which seemed odd for someone who was well-known for his singing and preaching ministry. On another seat I saw a well-known street-kids' worker. He seemed content, and was talking to others. On the third chair I saw a colleague in the ministry who had pioneered a church in Perth. He was sitting at a table with other people, laughing happily.

In a nutshell all three men represented something of my own life, gifts, talents and calling hiding under the car and wanting to come out. I readily understood that I was not the only one who was reluctant to express gifts and talents, and that many people hide away potential that is just longing to get out.

My friend from Perth reflected the pioneering aspect of my life that I was about to move into. The youth worker seemed to represent a part of my gifting as a youth communicator. The singer, without doubt, reflected the gift of singing that is in me that has become somewhat dormant in recent years.

WAR

People frequently dream about contending in battle. For some it may simply be the recalling of experiences from the time of their military service in war.

For most, however, it is likely to be a symbol of a battle occurring within themselves; perhaps a fight between good and evil intentions, the need to choose between right and wrong. Perhaps the dream is revealing an inner turmoil or deep-seated conflict.

The symbol of war will nearly always speak of a struggle, imprisonment or some form of restriction.

War, hate, greed and death are strongly associated with violence. When considering this, we may also need to consider whether there may be a need to forgive and restore certain relationships. I am reminded of the Apostle

Paul's words in the book of Romans 7:15-25. He speaks of an internal struggle between two natures, two attitudes. A fight between choosing good over evil, life over death. His comments are a little like a tongue twister. "I do not understand myself at all, for I really want to do what is right, but I can't. I do what I don't want to - what I hate. I know perfectly well that what I am doing is wrong, and my bad conscience proves that I agree with these laws I am breaking. But I can't help myself, because I'm no longer doing it. It is sin inside me (*old nature*) that is stronger than I am that makes me do these evil things... It seems to be a fact of life that when I want to do what is right, I inevitably do what is wrong. I love to do God's will so far as my *new nature* is concerned..." (Living Bible translation).

The Apostle Paul is a classic example in waking life, where two natures are at war within - one nature being evil and the other being good and godly. Such conflict can manifest itself in a dream during the night.

I once heard a pastor preach a wonderful message that I've titled 'Dog eat Dog'. He used an example of a missionary in India who had recently won a convert to the Lord. After some time he returned to see how the man was going in his newfound faith in the Lord. The missionary asked, "So how has your Christian walk been going?" The man replied, "It has been somewhat of a struggle. All of a sudden I have had a greater consciousness of what is good and what is evil. It has been as though two dogs have been at *war* within in me." The missionary asked, "Which one is winning?" The convert's immediate reply was, "The one I feed the most."

HEAVY ARTILLERY

I once dreamt of a row of tanks on the horizon, launching their shells at me. When they realised that no harm had come to me they then brought out larger guns and pointed them in my direction. At this alarming point, I woke up.

It was shortly after, I ran into some conflict with a workmate and was reminded of the dream. Instantly, I knew I must guard my heart and watch my attitude very closely. The dream I had had seemed to indicate a build up of intensity, going from smaller guns to larger guns, and that any reaction on my part most definitely had the potential for a war of words. Thankfully it was peacefully resolved.

TREE

A tree can be a symbol of both strength and weakness depending on the condition of the tree and context in which it is used.

In Nebuchadnezzar's dream he saw a tree stripped of its foliage, which symbolised loss and humility. But a loss of foliage could also represent a change of season in your life.

For Nebuchadnezzar, one minute the tree was high and mighty then it was reduced to a stump. (Daniel chapter 4).

A tall tree with much fruit can represent a pleasant outcome in the realm of prosperity and success, as was the case for King Nebuchadnezzar.

A tree can also stand for one's 'Family Tree'. I had just finished my last session in a dreams' seminar when I was approached by a man from another state. He told me about a dream he'd had about a tree.

THE FAMILY TREE

Both he and his brother were walking towards a large tree. The tree was full of various animals and it seemed odd for some of the creatures to be up the tree for it was not their normal habitat. He saw one of the creatures fall out of the tree.

I asked the Holy Spirit to reveal what the dream meant. After questioning the man about his brother, it became clear that their relationship had known better days. The tree and brother together represented his family. The animals reflected certain attitudes; some were good while others needed to be thrown out. I asked him whether he could remember what the creature looked like, that had fallen out of the tree. He replied that it was a gnawing type of animal. When I went to the dictionary I found specifically that gnawing means: To wear away by biting. The dream was telling this man that the gnawing attitude needed to be dealt with and thrown out. In turn the relationship between him and his brother would be restored. When I asked him if there was some attitude that was gnawing away at their relationship, he answered that there was.

ANIMALS

Animals may symbolise certain emotions, characteristics, attitudes and attributes. Again we need to ask questions about the animal. What type of creature is it? What is it known for? Is it domestic or dangerous, wild or tame? Is it on the prowl? Perhaps you are unaware of something sneaking up on you. God could use your pet to speak to you about loyalty or it may be symbolic of a 'pet' project. If you had a fear of *dogs* and in your dream you confidently approach one, the dream is possibly saying that you are overcoming an area of fear in your life. A *lion* may represent boldness, and confidence. Conversely, a lion may represent a destroyer or devourer. A *mule* often reflects stubbornness, but you might consider that it is a hybrid animal; one that is a product of two different species, and cannot reproduce.

A *horse* often is a creature used for transport. In the Bible it is often seen as the measure of strength of an army. It is also used in Revelations, usually bearing some mighty one on its back.

A *rat* could stand for something unclean. People often use the term, 'you dirty rat' when referring to someone who has betrayed or ill-used them.

A *pig* may mean a similar thing. It could stand for over-eating. (Not that any of us have trouble with that, do we?) You may find yourself casting pearls before swine; perhaps you are wasting your breath trying to help someone. It is also worth remembering that the pig or swine was considered one of the unclean animals in the Bible, and that the Jews were not permitted to eat their flesh, as it would make them unclean.

BIRDS

Birds can often symbolise freedom and the emotion associated with unrestricted flight. For Native Americans or even Christians, the eagle usually stands for spiritual knowledge and strength. The eagle is portrayed in the Bible as a symbol of strength and vision. "But those who hope in the Lord will renew their strength. They will soar on wings like eagles; they will run and not grow weary, they will walk and not be faint." Isaiah 40:31

A dove is often used as the symbol of the Holy Spirit but can also be interpreted as the need for a more gentle approach. Also, remember the dove brought back the olive leaf to Noah after the flood, indicating that the time of waiting and testing was nearly over.

Jesus speaks of a sparrow when he tells his followers not to be anxious about anything. He tells them that not one sparrow falls to the earth that the Father does not know about. Perhaps a sparrow is symbolic of God's ever-present care for us.

The ravens were sent by God to feed Elijah at a time when he was suffering from discouragement and severe depression. Perhaps the raven speaks of God caring for you during a time of emotional low.

The vulture might symbolise death, the owl wisdom, the peacock pride and vanity. What type of bird is it you've dreamed of and what is it doing? Is it caged, tied to a string, nesting or in full flight? Perhaps it's trying to get out of a room. What room and where is it?

There are so many species of birds that may represent so many different things. To a football player a bird might represent his team or club. Many of our sporting teams are named after birds and animals.

Birds may come up in a dream as metaphor, 'sitting duck' (open and vulnerable), 'chicken-hearted' (afraid and cowardly), 'cocky' (arrogant), turkey (stupid).

WEDDINGS

A symbol that I have been frequently approached about is a wedding. It is interesting to note that not everyone I talk to about weddings gets married in the dream.

I'M NOT SURE

I once met a lady from another state who shared a dream in which she saw herself walking down the aisle. On every occasion she would dream this, the dream would only ever consist of her just walking down the aisle, nothing else. In each instance it was difficult for her to make out who the groom was. In her waking life, she was in a steady relationship with a fellow, though she wasn't confident about marrying him. I felt the dream was confirming her feeling that she should not rush into something that she might regret.

I DO

On another occasion I spoke with a lady who was also in a steady relationship and found herself walking down the aisle in her dream. Every time she dreamed this same dream she was further down the aisle than before and eventually married the groom. Unlike the other lady, she greatly admired, loved and respected her man. To me, the dream was a confidence booster, encouraging her to pursue a life-long relationship and commitment to her man.

As is often said at the ceremony, marriage is not something a person should enter into lightly, but rather it is a life-long investment requiring careful thought and consideration. One must be cautious making a commitment to marry based on a dream. Be sure to take it slowly. Make it a matter of prayer, take wise counsel and advice from those who are close to you and people you trust.

I DON'T

A young lady I know had her boyfriend propose to her, but she was concerned that the relationship was accelerating too fast. Unsettled by this rushed feeling, she called the relationship off, and yet she couldn't help but wonder whether she had done the right thing. That night she dreamt she wore a wedding dress and yet there was no veil. The veil in this instance represented her covering. 1 Corinthians 11:10 speaks of a head covering or veil which was to symbolise the principle of spiritual covering and the order of headship in a relationship. "For this reason… the woman ought to have a sign of authority on her head." Having no veil on her head in the dream was confirming to her that she was yet to meet the right man who in time would be her appointed covering in life.

The symbol for wedding or marriage can be given other suggested interpretations. A wedding can speak of union, the coming together of an idea, project or dream. Divorce can speak of division, separation, split, disharmony, friction or disagreement.

A couple that came to me during a seminar spoke of dreaming the same thing on the same night. In their case I believe the dream was not metaphorical in nature, but rather it was literally addressing an area of boredom and dissatisfaction that existed in their marriage. I was able to sit with them and talk through the meaning of the dream. The Holy Spirit gave me some incredible insight into the dreams' symbolism and relevance for their relationship. We were able to prevent a potential extra-marital affair.

BABY

In my dream I was in hospital giving birth to a baby out of my mouth. Now that would make an interesting cartoon! Just prior to giving birth, the surgeon injected some anaesthetic into my mouth.

A baby nearly always represents a new beginning perhaps of an idea, a project or venture. As a preacher I am preoccupied with words; in this dream it seemed to be illustrating a fresh flow of truth, but contained a painkilling effect (anaesthetic), soothing, numbing and deadening the pain in people's lives.

Being pregnant can be symbolic of the period of incubation required for an idea or project to develop. Feeding a baby may suggest pouring more into an idea that is still in its infancy. However, there is always the possibility that one could literally be pregnant and not know it yet.

Should you find yourself abandoning a baby, perhaps you need to consider the saying, 'Don't throw the baby out with the bath water.' It may be indicative of throwing away not just the trials and obstacles that may present themselves, but actually throwing out the whole idea or project altogether.

If you should dream of several babies, ask yourself whether you have taken on too much.

To wake up from a dream of killing a baby can send someone into a cold sweat. Rather than panicking, ask yourself whether perhaps you have died to a certain idea, or maybe you've stepped out into a new venture and it hasn't worked out.

Though we could spend countless hours and energy on looking at symbol after symbol, I would suggest that most of the understanding will come from personal experience and the quest to interpret things as accurately as we can. It is essential that, like Joseph, we do not forget that "…interpretations of dreams belong to God." Genesis 40:8. Let us seek out the Maker and Giver of all wisdom.

YOU CAN'T JUDGE A BOOK BY ITS COVER, BUT THE COVER CAN TELL YOU QUITE A LOT ABOUT THE BOOK

Before we begin to look at the five laws of interpreting dreams, it is important to note the dream's theme. Understanding the theme will reduce the elements of the dream to their simplest form.

EVERY DREAM HAS A THEME

If I were to say, *Star Wars*, most would think of science fiction; a battle between the rebellion and the empire. If I said, *Jurassic Park,* most would think of dinosaurs. If I said, *Brave Heart,* most would think of William Wallace and his quest for freedom.

Imagine going to a movie theatre to watch a show, but you don't have any clue as to the story line before you go. No hint is given as to what the show is about, nor have you a clue to its title. Or in the same way, if you went to read a book, but found it had no title or front cover.

This is an analogy of what often happens when you dream. You are introduced to your own motion picture with yourself playing the leading role, but there is usually no title, nor are you introduced to a theme. Once a person discovers the theme of their dream, the rest of the process of interpretation seems to fall into line quite quickly.

Let's use one of my dreams to explore this a little further. Before interpreting any dream we need to remind ourselves to have a good look at what has been going on in our lives at the time.

I was very busy preparing for a one-week ministry trip to Queensland. My mother was down from the Gold Coast, staying with us for two weeks. Our next-door neighbours' marriage was on the rocks and the wife had spent the night at our place. As a result of all this activity, I was spending very little time with my wife, Kate.

Perhaps as you read about this dream you may be able to tell me what its theme is. Be sure to stop as soon as you have read it. Try not to read my interpretation, but spend a moment working out what *you* would title this dream:

I dreamt that I'd just woken up. The bedroom curtains were open and I saw two unshaven workmen just outside the window, peering into our bedroom. I nudged Kate with my elbow, but she was watching T.V. "Won't someone close the curtains. Look at the way those guys are looking into our room," I said, annoyed that she was ignoring me. I got out of bed and drew the curtains, but the workmen were still trying to have a peek.

INTERPRETATION

Sometimes in a seminar I ask everybody to try and come up with the theme of this brief drama. If it was a movie and I wanted to arouse enough curiosity for people to see it, what would I title it? Here are a few of the many replies I've received: 'Peeping Tom'; 'TV or not TV'; 'Bedroom Boredom'. Personally, I think that the title, 'Invasion of Privacy' describes it the best. Now that we have identified the theme, what about the symbols?

The scene took place in the bedroom, which could reflect the intimate side of my relationship with Kate. Not realising it, the pace of my work life (*workmen outside trying to peer in*) was beginning to take its toll, biting into the time I would normally spend with my wife. The *unshaven men* symbolised the element of neglect on my part, allowing the increased pace in my work life to eat into our personal time together. *Kate watching the TV,* which we don't actually have in our bedroom, symbolised the emotional tender and caring part of my life (*Kate),* that was not responding because it was being distracted by the TV. In my dream, I was looking for Kate to close the curtain, when all along it was my responsibility to close the door to busyness and disruption.

It is important to mention that the feeling tone of the dream was one of frustration.

As soon as I'd thought all this through, I immediately approached my wife and asked her whether she felt I was neglecting her. After a little discussion, I decided to mend my ways, and she, as always, was wonderfully forgiving. I took her out to dinner that night and closed the curtain on that short chapter of my life.

BACK IN BRITAIN

Another example of a theme can be found in the dream of a young English visitor. He was spending three months with our church in Australia. We asked him several times whether he would consider playing keyboard for our annual History Makers Youth Conference. He had made prior arrangements and so apologised that he was unable to help. A little later, one morning in my office, he began to share a recurring dream that he had been having over a period of two weeks.

"I dream I'm back in England in my flat, and I find myself packing to go to Australia."

It was a simple dream with a simple message. The main question was, what was the theme of this dream. I knew it to be important as it kept recurring. He asked me what I thought it meant, but I had to say that I didn't know at that point. However, we prayed and asked the Holy Spirit to help us. The young man was somewhat perplexed as he couldn't understand why he was back in England packing, when he was already living in Australia.

I began to pace my office, thinking, praying, asking, what the theme might be? I did wonder what this young man must have thought as I was pacing and muttering to myself. "What's the theme? Packing! He's packing, but he's packing back in England. Doesn't make sense, he's here in Australia." Again I paced some more, prayed, paced, and prayed. Eventually, I asked him what it was he was packing. He told me it was just clothes and stuff, the gear you normally pack. The only thing that seemed clear to me was that the theme simply revolved around packing, but then I asked myself a question that flicked the switch. Why do we pack? Obvious! We pack things we are going to use when we get there. At this point I became quite excited. I believed the Holy Spirit was shedding some light on the subject. Quickly I asked him another question about what he hadn't packed when he'd come here. Was there something in the dream that he'd been packing but had actually forgotten to bring? It suddenly seemed to me that he'd gone back to England in the dream to pack something that he'd thought he wasn't going to use. I asked him once again, "Is there anything in your dream that you were packing which you might have overlooked?"

I will never forget what happened next. With tears in his eyes he looked at me and said, "I was packing a keyboard, and it was your church's keyboard." I asked him if he thought he knew what it meant. Instantly he responded, "I need to play keyboard for History Makers, that's why I have had the same dream for two weeks. The Lord has been trying to get through to me."

He stayed for that week and played, and his friend from England re-scheduled his flight to Melbourne to join us.

By the way, the other item the young man packed in his dream was a computer. He went on to compile all the music sheets for our church's CD that we had produced that year.

So there we have it! Find the theme for your dream!

CHAPTER 6

Five laws to interpretation

*Visions and dreams are the language of the
fourth dimension, and the Holy Spirit
communicates through them.*[1]
Dr. Paul Yonggi Cho

FIVE LAWS FOR INTERPRETING YOUR DREAMS

I have given considerable thought and prayer to presenting a simple series of steps that people can use to help interpret their dreams. One day while driving to Sydney it came to me. I believe the Holy Spirit inspired me with the following five principles that make up the acronym DREAM.

D iscern whether the dream is literal or metaphorical.

R ecent concerns and events.

E xamine the feeling tone.

A sk for insight.

M ake sure the interpretation sits well with the dreamer.

D - Discern whether the dream is literal or metaphorical

The dream should always be considered literal in the first instance and examined for signs of impending danger or signs that simply remind us of things unattended to. Perhaps you have lost an article and dream of where you last left it and so on. If the dream makes no sense when taken literally, then it is quite possibly a metaphorical statement of the dreamer's feelings at the time of the dream.

I remember reading an article in the Readers Digest that a certain lady awoke from an afternoon catnap. She awoke distressed, having dreamt a person was drowning. Knowing the next-door neighbours had a swimming pool, she dashed out, and peering over the fence saw the neighbour's child floating on top of the water. She immediately jumped the fence and rescued the young girl just in time. Thank God for a lady who took a dream seriously and literally enough to check just in case. This is a clear-cut example of where a dream applies to its literal context rather than metaphorical.

I hadn't been home long from conducting a 'dream' seminar in Melbourne when I received an email from the co-ordinator of the function. This was another example where the dream applied literally and she was pleasantly surprised. "I had an amazing dream the other week," she wrote. "I must tell you. I dreamt I did a pregnancy test and it came up positive. It was so vivid, I needed to check into it. I remember learning from you to check the literal first, so I did that. And guess what? I am pregnant!! Nine weeks on. Isn't God great!"

R - Recent concerns and events

The Bible tells us that dreams are triggered off by certain events and circumstances that may occur in any given day. Earlier I quoted from Ecclesiastes 5:3 where it reminded us that dreams arise out of cares and concerns, and the general business of day to day life. It's very important to know the person's background and current events surrounding the individual's life. Ask some questions: How is family life? Has anything significant taken place lately? Is there anything troubling you?

The questions should always revolve around the context of the dream. I would be very hesitant to try and interpret anyone's dreams without this knowledge.

E - Examine your mood and the emotion of the dream

The feeling tone, or emotion in the dream will shed more light on its meaning.

For example if the feeling tone of the dream is miserable, then the dream was more than likely sparked off by some miserable situation in life. You may dream that chaos is breaking out all around you, yet the feeling tone is one of calm and security. Perhaps you are in for a trying and testing time and the dream is revealing that calmness and composure will help you ride it out.

Feelings of hesitation and suspicion can communicate uncertainty. Be sure to ask yourself how you felt in the dream.

When my children were younger I used to play a game with them called *Hide and Seek*. It's not the type of game where someone counts to ten and the other hides. Our version is a little different. In this game there's only one player, much like when you dream there is also only one player. I blindfold one of my children and make thoroughly sure they can't see. Once blindfolded, I give them an object, it might be anything from a spoon to a pen, or one of their toys. They take the item in their hands and by touching the object, moving it around and concentrating on the *feel* of it, attempt to identify it correctly. This can be a lot of fun, you ought to try it.

Dreams are a little like this. We too are blindfolded by our sleep.

Many of our dreams contain strong emotion and identifying the feeling tone can give you a great deal more insight and understanding into the dream.

A - Ask the Holy Spirit to reveal the meaning behind the symbols.

Why should we inquire of the Lord? For the same reason Daniel did. He realised his need to seek God for meanings to the mysteries. Daniel 2:28 "But there is a God in heaven who reveals mysteries..." Matthew 7:7 further encourages us that he who seeks, finds.

M - Make sure the interpretation of the dream is freeing and releasing

In the vast majority of cases a dream is correctly interpreted when it makes sense to the dreamer in terms of the person's present life and situation, and when it moves them to change his or her life for the better. Generally, a dream correctly interpreted will not leave the dreamer confused and bewildered.

There are situations and circumstances where a dream and its interpretation may unsettle a person by conviction and challenge. Though not common, a dream can warn of an unpleasant outcome.

The story recorded in Genesis 40, tells of two men who were both put into prison for offending their master, the king of Egypt. Both asked Joseph to interpret a dream each had had. The cupbearer was pleased to hear Joseph say that his dream foretold he would be released in three days. However, the baker's interpretation was not so positive. Joseph told him that in three days he would be hung from a tree. In this case Joseph's interpretation possibly didn't sit well with the dreamer. All I can say in this instance is be careful whom you offend. Offending your friend can be one thing, but to offend the king of Egypt, well, I think we get the picture.

If you should have a distressing dream, I would advise you to bring the matter before the Lord in prayer and if there is need for humility, do what is necessary to set things straight.

The example of the baker's dream is an exception, when the majority of dreams usually are an assortment of our day-to-day activities and serve as a releasing mechanism, and not something that binds and confuses.

Let me give you an example of how the five laws work. I had just finished a session on 'Dreams and Visions' at a youth conference. As the two hundred young people began to move out of the crowded seminar room, I noticed two teenage girls who sat opposite me. One girl asked if she could tell me about a dream she'd had. Her friend was sitting quietly next to her in support.

MUM, STOP IT!

"I dreamt I was at home in the backyard going down the slide. I walked into the house and found my nine-year-old sister under the table scribbling on the family photos. She was destroying them."

At this point the girl started to cry, and we waited while her friend comforted her. After she regained her composure, she continued.

"I saw my sister carving away at the photos and I turned to mum who was in the kitchen. I said, 'Mum, please stop her! Stop her, Mum!'"

The girl told me that in her dream her mother had not shown any interest, almost as if she didn't care. She didn't do anything to stop the little sister.

INTERPRETATION BY USING THE FIVE LAWS

Here is how I used the five laws to help me interpret the girl's dream.

D Discern whether the dream is literal or metaphorical.

In this case it was clear that this was a metaphorical dream. It was symbolic in nature, needing insight and understanding.

R Recent concerns and events

What fascinated me about this young lady was that she cried when telling me the dream, which is not common. I asked her to repeat the dream once more and as she did she began to cry again. On both occasions she broke down crying when she referred to her sister destroying the photos. I asked her how things were in her life. She replied that they were OK. Her answer was not particularly convincing and I realised that my question had been a general one. I asked more specifically how her family life was. Her response was that it could be better. She told me that her mother and she were not talking.

I noticed that she was still emotionally overwhelmed by the dream (feeling tone). It was obvious to me that the dream was a reflection of her home life. I felt confident by asking her these questions, that I had accumulated reasonable background information.

One must exercise sensitivity and proceed carefully and gently with some people.

E Evaluate the mood and emotions of the dream.

Even as I heard the girl speak about her dream I could detect feelings of frustration coupled with anger, resentment and even distress. The feeling tone is very important, and here it was so intense that it caused her to cry as she told me her dream.

A Ask the Holy Spirit to reveal the meanings behind the symbols.

My heart really went out to this young girl. I could see that her home life brought great distress. Struggling to find the key that fitted the lock, I asked the Holy Spirit to give me a breakthrough in understanding the symbols.

WHAT COULD THESE SYMBOLS MEAN?

The Lord began to unfold the meaning to her dream. I saw how the photos were symbolic of memories. Going down the slide was indicative of how she felt about her mother. She cried in the dream pleading with her mother to please stop it.

She was distressed at the thought that all the fond memories amounted to nothing and that for two years it was as though things of the past didn't matter. The daughter had bottled up her emotions for so long and hadn't told anyone of the situation, hoping that her mother would bring an end to the rift. She'd found it difficult to talk to her father because she did not want to complicate matters any further. The young lady assured me upon returning home that she would talk to her dad and see how her relationship with her mother could be restored.

M Make sure the interpretation is freeing and releasing

Your interpretation to any dream must leave a sense of 'Ah, yes, of course!' Only the dreamer knows whether the interpretation to the dream is correct. In Genesis 40:12 Joseph interprets the cupbearer's dream. Some time later in Genesis 41:25-39 he is standing before Pharaoh interpreting his dream. In both cases the dream's interpretation was well received.

Not only did King Nebuchadnezzar favourably receive Daniel's interpretation to his dream (Daniel 2:46), but in the very next verse, we see how God was using the dream to draw the King's heart to Himself. He acknowledged "Surely your God is the God of gods and the Lord of Kings and a revealer of mysteries…"

Allow the interpretation to sit with the dreamer and ask them things like: how does this line up? Could it mean this? It may be saying that.

Caution needs to be taken in assuming that your interpretation is correct without checking it with the person involved.

I asked the girl whether the interpretation seemed right to her. Did it make any sense? Crying once again she said, "Yes, very much."

These five principles have proved to be immensely helpful to so many, and I hope they will for you too. Consider another quick example.

PINS AND NEEDLES

A man during a workshop session shared a dream he'd had. Everybody else was encouraged to play a part in the interpretation of it. I do stress that this is a very personal exercise, and you need to realise that you become vulnerable in doing so. There is every chance the dream may unfold certain thoughts of a private nature.

"I dreamt that I was walking along the road next to the beach with my daughter. It was during an access visit. A truck drove by and dumped some needles in front of me. I walked straight into them. They were all over me. I was fearful at the thought of my daughter pulling them out one by one. Most of the needles were smaller though some were bigger. Every time my daughter would pull a needle out it brought relief."

INTERPRETATION

By using the five principles I asked the people whether they were able to shed light on the dream.

D   It was evident the dream was metaphorical in nature rather than literal.

R   He was divorced from his wife; his daughter was thirteen years of age. One of the ladies involved in the church prayer team suggested the dream be titled, 'Pins and Needles'. The people were fantastic and the whole exercise was handled with sensitivity and care. There was no doubt in the minds of those present that the dream was related to the break up with his wife.

E   His feelings were overwhelmed by the dump of emotions as they were unloaded on his life. These were followed by feelings of relief as, one by one, each situation was dealt with.[2]

A   The symbolism of the needles could reflect the numbness, like the 'pins and needles', that the separation from his wife had caused. The daughter was part of the plan in the healing process, as one issue at a time she was able to help in restoring her father's life. Some of the needles (pain) were driven deep and some only shallow, indicating that he would get over some issues quicker than others.

M   I asked the man how he felt about what was said. It was quite evident that he was impressed by the relevance of everyone's thoughts.

CHAPTER 7

Common Dreams

"Is it not known to all people that the dream is the most usual way that God reveals himself to man?"

Tertullian

NINE COMMON 'DREAM THEMES'

DREAM THEME 1: FALLING

The first step is to see whether or not the dream contains some kind of warning of a possible literal fall in your life. For example, a certain man dreamt that his son fell off a ladder. Upon examining his ladder he discovered a loose rung. The father attended to the matter and prevented a possible fall from occurring.

If the dream is not literal then one should consider the possibility of a metaphorical meaning. Dreams where a person is falling could indicate that the dreamer is not on solid ground, or perhaps a loss of control. It might even be an instance of 'falling from grace', as was the case of a young Catholic girl who had slept with her boyfriend and later felt ashamed.

The fear of falling can often reflect being overwhelmed with feelings of insecurity or inadequacy, as was the case when I dreamed just before a trip to Taiwan.

THE TRIP TO TAIWAN

I was scheduled to fly out to Taiwan to work with an experienced and successful healing evangelist. This was to be my first trip on a venture such as this.

Several nights prior to departure I dreamt I boarded the plane for Taiwan. On route the plane started to dive rather suddenly, and I was concerned though not fearful.

When I woke from the dream my first thought was whether I should cancel the trip or not. Then upon close examination of my feelings, I concluded that the plane falling was a reflection of my feelings of insecurity. I wasn't fearful, rather concerned that I wouldn't match up to the ministry expectations in Taiwan.

I ended up going and highly valued the experience and the opportunities of ministering on a new level.

After conducting a 'Dreams and Visions' seminar in another state, I was pleased to see one of my old friends come up to speak to me. He began to tell me about a dream he'd had.

HANDS UP

He had dreamt he was falling, only his arms were raised and he had begun to praise the Lord. While he was praising God in his dream, he noticed he'd begun to slow down. But every time he'd bring his arms to his side he would begin to fall at great speed again. So he lifted his arms up in worship to the Lord again and found himself slowing down for a safe and secure landing.

My friend recognised the dream as a reflection of his feeling insecure about some things and as he looked to the Lord, and by casting his cares on Him (1Peter 5:7), he was reassured that all would be well, safe and secure.

This whole dream reminded me of the time Moses was on the mountain top as the Israelites were in the heat of battle with the Amalekites (Exodus 17:11). As long as Moses had his hands lifted up the Israelites were winning, but whenever he lowered them they were losing. The message is quite clear as it reveals our need to look to the Lord in our every circumstance.

My friend is not the only one who has ever suffered from feelings of insecurity. I dare say that it is quite common, but the message he derived from his dream can bring an encouragement to us all. In times of fear, trial and insecurity, don't fold your arms in self-defence or defiance, but lift them to the God who knows and loves you.

Perhaps you will find yourself coming in for a *safe* and *secure* landing.

DO YOU DIE IF YOU FALL TO THE GROUND?

This is but an old wives' tale and is nothing more than a myth. There have been accounts of people who have dreamt they fell to the bottom and have lived to tell their skydiving stories. So relax and enjoy the view on your way down.

I'll never forget the night my wife had a falling dream in the early hours of the morning. But it was not just a mental picture only in her mind; I mean it was a literal falling dream. I was violently shaken from my sleep as I heard my wife scream out, "Oh no!" She dived out of the bed, plunged her knee into my stomach, before landing on the floor on my side of the bed. "What in the world was that all about?" I asked, somewhat shaken. "The pot was falling off the stove," she answered.

Now before someone asks the question, was there any meaning to her dream, I must hastily inform you: No! It was just a simple case of a husband who nearly hit the ceiling in fright.

DREAM THEME 2: FLYING

Most people I meet have enjoyed the dream of feeling weightless as they fly like a bird. Some of us have known what it means to be 'faster than a speeding bullet, more powerful than a locomotive and able to leap tall buildings in a single bound'. Superman has nothing on our experiences. I bet those movie producers would love to know how to create the special effects that so many of us experience in our dreams.

Dreams of flying express the feeling of being 'high' or 'on top of the world', or perhaps 'rising above' circumstances or avoiding restrictions or even avoiding responsibility. Once again, the feeling tone of either elation or anxiety gives the clue as to how you really feel about these events in your life. The height you fly to can sometimes be important. It may suggest a promotion is on the way, a climbing to a new level.

The week prior to catching my flight out to a conference, I had a dream that I was flying. I hadn't experienced this exhilaration of flying since childhood. To me the dream was confirming a new level of prophetic ministry that I was about to come into at this coming conference.

Flying dreams can also indicate a sense of trying to escape from real life, or wishful thinking. Remember that every dream is personal, and its symbols and metaphorical meaning must sit right with the dreamer.

DREAM THEME 3: RUNNING:

It's not uncommon for people to dream that they're running yet getting nowhere: the type of feeling where your legs feel like lead and what you're running from is quickly gaining on you.

Perhaps the question is: what are you running from that you need to confront in your life? What is it that's trying to catch up with you that you're neglecting? Perhaps you're running to catch a ferry to get to the other side and you're afraid if you don't make it you'll 'miss the boat'.

This type of dream may also be highlighting the need to run from temptation. In 1 Corinthians 6:18, 1Timothy 6:11 and James 4:7, we are encouraged to flee from certain things that are harmful and damaging to our lives.

My first dream ever recorded in my journal in the early eighties, in retrospect seems to have been the catalyst; the gateway into the world of dreams; definitely a defining moment in my life.

SEE YOU AT THE TOP:

It was a wide road, which narrowed off into the distance, with thick forest on either side of it. I found myself running with thousands of other people. It almost felt over-crowded yet comfortable. Though we all ran for some time no one seemed tired and each appeared 'fit for the task'. As I looked into the distance it was clear to me that everyone was making his or her way to an enormous mountain. In the frustration of not being able to get there quickly enough, I took a right turn into the forest, hoping the short cut would save time. Not only did this slow me down but also I became frightened as I noticed gorillas all around me. Without hesitation my feet made their way back to the road.

Finally the road had connected with the mountain. As I looked up there were thousands of ropes hanging from the peak to the foot of this great climb. Grabbing hold of a rope I commenced the climb, all along wondering who was at the top. It wasn't long before I overtook the large crowd of climbers and looking down I was amazed at two things. Firstly, there wasn't anyone near me within at least 500 metres; secondly, I was amazed to see so many making the journey.

At last I had reached the top, with one arm over the edge trying to lever my way up. It was proving a little difficult until I noticed one of my youth leaders, who at that time was Pastor Nick Resce. "Take my hand, I'll help you up," he said. Lifting me up and over I finally made it with my feet safe and secure on the top. I couldn't believe my eyes. I was standing on a flat surface; the whole mountain was a sheet of glass. Nick took me to the Youth Pastor, and we both turned to see a helicopter approaching us from the horizon. It hovered above us before landing. I wondered why there was no pilot. The Youth Pastor escorted me into the helicopter and said: "You'll have to go but we will see you again." He waved as I took off into the sunrise.

The dream was quite a marathon in more ways than one. In this case I was not running from, but rather running to. What I was running to was a meeting with my destiny. A brief outline of the dream will help in understanding it.

Road: – The path of life, a journey.

The crowd: – 'Many are called, few are chosen' Matthew 22:14

Short cut: – Feelings of frustration

Forest: – It's dense. Couldn't see (loss of direction), which actually slowed me down. If I had persisted in the forest the **gorillas** would have sabotaged my destiny.

Ropes: – Someone was up there, though I didn't know who or what.

Top of the mountain: – Only people who were prepared to pay the price arrived there. There were many on the bottom giving consideration to whether they should or shouldn't commence the climb. The top was like a **sheet of glass** – you have to be transparent with God. Only people with upright hearts, integrity and honesty were welcomed there.

Pastor Nick Resce: – It was only a few years later that Nick was the one who invited me into full-time ministry. He gave me a hand up in the dream and actually has done so in real life several times since.

Youth Pastor: – He sent me off into the sunrise. The sun rises in the east, and it wasn't long afterwards that I set off eastwards to New South Wales, Sydney, to do my Discipleship Training School with YWAM.

Helicopter: – Reminded me of God the Holy Spirit. You can't see him (no pilot), who hovers above Genesis 1:2 '…and the Spirit of God was hovering…'

This running dream turned out to be one of the most important dreams of my life, confirming the reality of the call of God on my life to full time ministry. In this case I was running to something - something great. As in this dream, climbing heights can speak of promotion and promise.

One time I dreamt that I'd hopped off my pushbike and was walking it up this steep hill. It seemed a tiresome climb, but upon reaching the top, I got back on the bike and began to pedal again.

In this case climbing represented a process, long term, that was not necessarily going to happen overnight. It can speak of the need for endurance and discipline. I once heard a preacher say: "It's just as easy to walk on top of the mountain as it is at the bottom. It's getting there that takes time and energy."

DREAM THEME 4: NUDITY

Anna Farraday in her book "The Dream Game" shares some helpful insights on the subject.
"It is widely believed that dreams of being naked or scantily clad in public are indications of sexual feelings or guilt about sex, but the truth is that in most cases such dreams have no reference to sex at all, and even those that do, often have only an incidental concern with it. In the first place, such dreams can be literal warnings of something wrong with your clothes - and if you dream of finding yourself naked at an airport, do check that you have packed your pants for tomorrow's journey! If all is well at this level, then you must ask in what way you feel naked, revealed, vulnerable, exposed, or open in your life at this present time."

This has got to be one of the best explanations on the subject of nudity in dreams. She gives an example in the following dream:

EXPOSED

"A university lecturer had a recurring dream in which he was walking through the college grounds and reading in the library, when he suddenly senses all eyes upon him. Looking down, he discovers to his dismay that he is naked or clad only in shoes and socks.

As the dream takes place in college, it obviously refers to some aspect of work, and he is able to relate it to the fact that he blatantly uses other people's ideas to advance himself, a habit he consciously thinks is rather clever. The dream, however, which usually occurs as soon as he's published a paper, expresses his heart's fears that this time he is sure to be found out and *exposed* as a fraud - and the dream will no doubt re-occur until he gets head and heart on this issue."[1]

A young high school student, shared with me a recurring dream he often had. He said the dream stopped when he moved to his current Christian high school. He would dream that at the previous school he was naked, running and trying to find a place to hide.

In actual fact, some students in his previous school had taunted him, causing him to feel insecure and intimidated. Having no clothing on in his dream was a reflection of how he'd felt while at that school - exposed, isolated and cut off. Once he changed schools, the dream stopped. The students at the new school were welcoming and friendly to him.

GETTING IT OFF YOUR CHEST

I remember a dream where we'd invited a couple over for dinner. He was talking to me but had his shirt off baring his chest. I was facing him and I smiled, and took my shirt off, baring my chest as well. We shook hands. (Please don't get any wrong ideas; it's just a dream)

The dream was prompting me to settle a disagreement on a certain matter with a particular person I knew. He had a strong opinion on a certain issue, which differed from my opinion on the same matter, though I'd kept my view to myself. After the dream, we invited the man and his wife over for dinner. I took the opportunity to express my view on the matter. Initially, I had been reluctant to express my thoughts, thinking it would cause friction between us. But our relationship with these people was more important to me than this difference in opinion and so we talked until we'd arrived at a mutual agreement.

The dream was encouraging me to get the thing off my chest.

Dreams of nakedness can also indicate a lack of preparation; that a person is not ready for the job ahead, and some more effort is required in getting dressed for the occasion.

DREAM THEME 5: HOUSE

I have heard it quoted that around 40% of our dreams are about houses.

Again, if we dream something has broken down or there are signs of damage or general disrepair it would pay to investigate it literally, however, if all is well in that area then one should proceed to investigate the possibility of metaphorical content.

It's important to note that a house, in most cases, is a reflection of your life. The Bible sheds light on that when it refers to us being "the temple of the Holy Spirit." (1 Corinthians 3:16)

A house might refer to our body, personality, or character. The basement, living room, or attic can each represent an area of our life. Consider the following example of a young girl who was puzzled at a dream she had.

BEHIND CLOSED DOORS

She dreamt she was in the attic, and it was dark. Her grandmother was there and without warning, a black cat leapt out from behind her and began to tear into the girl's flesh. Suddenly her mother appeared and the cat vanished.

I'd known this girl for a while, and I'd always felt there was a dark side to her life. When she shared this dream with me, it seemed a great opportunity to talk with her. I outlined the dream for her as follows.

Attic: – resembled a place of storage in her life where one could hide things.

Dark: – It was dark, which could indicate something you didn't want people to see or know about.

Grandmother: – Whatever had been in the attic had been there for some time and may assume a friendly and welcoming front. The grandmother could also represent something that had been part of the family for generations.

Black Cat: – In this case it seemed to be something evil, coming from behind her, prowling and cutting away at her flesh.

Flesh: – The Bible has a lot to say about the flesh, it often being symbolic of sin. Flesh may not always mean sin in a dream, but in the context of this dream, I believed that was what it represented. It is interesting the cat came from behind. I recall Jesus saying to the Apostle Peter that the devil's place in life is behind Him (Matthew 16:23).

Mother: – Probably symbolises the girl's authority figure. When the mother came the cat vanished. Once the attic (hidden thing) was exposed to her mum, the evil thing disappeared.

When I asked the young lady whether the dream was painting a true picture of her life she said yes, though she was very reluctant to discuss the hidden agenda.

It was about two or three years later that she called and my fears were confirmed when she told me about the dark and troubled lifestyle she was leading.

There are many more dreams about houses. It is essential to understand the dream's theme, as this will establish what it is trying to say. In this case the theme was 'Hidden and Dark'.

In other instances, it is a possibility that the house could represent the house of the Lord, which refers to His church.

DREAM THEME 6: TEETH

There was a time where I was grinding my teeth in my dreams so badly, that they would crumble into a powdery form. In response to these dreams I arranged for a check up with my dentist, and he noticed my back teeth developed sharp edges to them. As he worked to round them off, he suggested I live more of a stress-free lifestyle. You would be wise to first treat a dream about teeth literally and see if they need attention. In my case the dream was telling me to attend to my problem both literally and emotionally.

CUTTING EDGE

While conducting a seminar in Queensland, a woman told me of her dream.

"It's quite simple," she said. *"I keep dreaming that I'm losing my teeth. What could this mean?"*

A fellow minister had suggested that she could be losing her cutting edge. This didn't seem to sit quite right with her. She then proceeded to ask me what I thought. I took some time to pray before getting back to her.

The Bible has a few things to say about the new and the old, for instance you can't pour new wine into old wineskins.(Matthew 9:17)

I believe that God, in her dream, was saying the same thing by using the symbol of teeth to convey the meaning. The Bible teaches us

COMMON DREAMS | 115

that the old always gives way to the new. Your new teeth will give you the cutting edge for what it is that you want to sink them into.

This woman responded to this interpretation very well, and told me how it reflected exactly where her life was. She felt that she was in transition between the old and the new in her life. The dream also further confirmed an encouragement she'd received earlier, about her coming into something new.

Another lady told me that she'd dreamt of having false teeth.

The dream could have been a warning concerning an element of falsehood in her life, or perhaps in what she had been saying; gossip or white lies.

If your teeth are healthy, ask yourself what you've felt during the dream and this will give you a clue to the meaning. While the symbol of teeth can mean different things to different people here are some suggestions.

Grinding Teeth:	stress, anger
False Teeth:	falsehood
Infected Teeth:	foul language, aggression (back biting), careless speech.
Wisdom Teeth:	could reflect wise choice or foolish
Baby Teeth:	immaturity, lacking experience
Loose baby teeth:	something new and more mature coming through
Loose Adult teeth:	something is threatened. Once you lose an adult tooth, that's it!

DREAM THEME 7: DEATH

There is an age-old belief that dreams can foretell impending death. This is certainly not true of the majority of dreams about people dying. If it were, I would have passed on long ago.

Often a dream about death is an expression that our feeling for someone, or their feeling for us, is dead. It may also show that we have allowed something in our inner life to die.

To dream of someone who has passed away is to dream what he or she used to, and may still, represent to us.

One of the most significant dreams about death is when we dream of our own death. This could be indicative of a dying to an area of our own life and perhaps the birth of something new and fresh. Perhaps it's related to a change in relationships or vocation, or perhaps it's the wrapping up of one chapter of your life and the beginning of a new one.

Author Jeremy Taylor sheds further light on the topic of death in dreams, in his book *Dream Work*.

"In my experience, all dream deaths are related at one level or another to the growth and transformation of personality. It is as though the old structure of personality which is being altered as a result of increasing maturity must die in order to make way for the new."[2]

Children often have nightmares or dream of death and dying. Childhood years change so quickly these types of dreams can often be associated with the child growing out of certain fears and insecurities. In the case where the child dreams of the death of his or her parents this could symbolise growing in an area of personal confidence, not being so dependent on the parents.

DEATH OF A FRIEND

When I was living in Adelaide, one of our church leaders had a dream.

She dreamt that while on my way to a conference, I had a car accident and died.

She woke up and phoned my wife to tell her to stop me from going. You can imagine the fear this brought to Kate. I must admit an anxious thought crossed my mind as well.

I considered carefully this leader's dream. To us she was more than just a church worker; she was also a close friend of the family. My sister and I had grown quite close to her as we'd come to know her family, and her genuine love and care became a great source of strength to us.

In the end, I had a peace about attending the conference, and I felt the dream had more to do with her life than mine, although I did not know how. It wasn't until I'd returned from the conference that I realised how significant the dream was for both of us.

It was while I was at the conference that I made the decision to move on from our church in Adelaide and take up a position with the Apostolic church in Geelong. The dream was telling of an end (death) that was coming to the relationship that we had developed over the years. It acted also as a confirmation for myself as well, when considering the enormous changes involved in a move interstate.

DEATH OF A LOVED ONE

I remember dreaming of the death of my father. In each instance it proved to be symbolic, representing an aspect of my father's life that was coming to an end in my own life.
If you should dream your father is dying it may concern the neglect of your fatherly role.

I remember a husband dreaming that his wife had died and that he was beside himself not knowing what he would do with his three young children.

It turned out that he was a passive type of father who left the whole parenting responsibility to his wife. I pointed out to him that he was abdicating his role in the home by leaving it solely to his wife. She was a capable and competent woman who carried much of the leadership in the house. His wife dying in the dream was symbolic of the leadership qualities in his life that were dead and dormant that needed to come to life.

It's also possible that parents whose children are moving out of the home, perhaps getting married or moving interstate, may dream the death of their child. Depending on the nature of the dream it could be prompting you to pray for them and for protection for them from danger.

On another occasion, while conducting a seminar, a woman asked me a question. "What happens when you dream you are standing next to your mother's coffin looking at her?"

I learned that her mother had died in New Zealand and she had been unable to make it to the funeral. I told her I believed the dream was giving her an opportunity to grieve properly over her mother's death and that she had felt deprived at not being able to attend. She began to cry, as did others around her. There was an incredible atmosphere of healing. I offered to pray for anyone who had suffered a loss in their life and who were still emotionally affected by it, and there were a lot of people who responded.

DREAM THEME 8: SEXUALITY

This is a sensitive topic and for good reason; it is the most intimate and private of all topics. I was hesitant to include the symbol of sexuality in this book, as it is not a subject generally approached by Christian authors. But I was reminded that an entire book of the Bible was devoted to this symbol in Song of Solomon, and was encouraged to include the following information.

Herman Riffel offers some sound insight on the subject: "Some of the most confusing dreams are sexual ones. They are often misunderstood because of the sex symbols involved, even though sexual dreams are usually not speaking of the physical expression of sex at all. Since God intended sexual relations to be the most intimate physical union of man and woman, the sexual dream is often used to describe the intimate union of the masculine and feminine parts of the personality."[3]

Perhaps this can be explained best by looking at some examples.

OBSESSION

A young man came to me with a concern that many of his dreams were filled with indecent acts and lustful scenes. When I asked him whether he had been reading or viewing things that were of a sexually explicit nature, he said yes. It didn't take long before I discovered from him that he had a compulsive need to sleep with different women, in addition to his addiction to the magazines he was reading and videos he was watching. I told him his night-time was no different to his daytime.

Herman Riffel further explains, "Unfortunately, the person who has turned his imagination to lustful thoughts becomes so dominated by them that no creative thought, especially one represented by a sexual symbol, can come via the dream... Some erotic dreams are innocent expressions of proper physical release. Lack of understanding of the normality and function of this kind of dream often produces false guilt."[4]

Anna Farraday conveys her thoughts on the subject: "Sex is like any other dream theme. It has a literal meaning if it reveals something about your actual sex feelings towards real people in your life at the time of the dream, but otherwise has to be understood as a *metaphor* for being 'excited', 'worked up', 'turned on', 'intimately involved', 'frustrated', 'deflated', or 'intruded upon'. It may refer to a cause you are 'embracing', an idea you are 'getting close to', or the 'coming together' of two aspects of your personality. In these cases the metaphor does not tell you how you see sex, but how much libido (energy, drive) you have invested in something in your life."[5]

NOT AS IT SEEMS

During a seminar a lady came up to me and thanked me so much for covering the area of sexuality in dreams. Over the years she'd had recurring dreams of sexual encounters with her brother and had been greatly distressed over the images. She said that her relationship with her brother had been *distant* and they'd been at odds with each other. She loved her brother very much and wished that things between them would be resolved. She was overjoyed to realise the dream was reflecting her desire to bridge the gap in their relationship and embrace the *closeness* they once knew. The dream was not literal, rather a metaphor or symbol of a strong desire to restore her relationship with her brother. It's easy to see how a dream like this could make a person feel awkward and uncomfortable. Some wake up feeling disgusted to think they would have dreamed such an act. Of all the symbols, the symbols of sexuality, if not understood, can lead to all sorts of confusion and self-condemnation.

TWO TIMER OR NO TIME

A certain lady dreamt that her husband was making love to another woman. She started to choke the lady and was very upset and rejected her husband.

She sat down with her husband and talked over the troubling dream. The woman was satisfied her husband wasn't in an adulterous relationship. The woman she was choking in her dream was the playmate aspect of her life that had been rejecting the advances her husband had been making. Without realising it she was slowly suffocating that side of her relationship with her husband.

The sexual symbol in its purest form is perhaps the most readily misunderstood. When such dreams are understood, instead of bringing guilt and shame, they bring a sense of relief.

IN BED WITH A MINISTER

Another woman, who recently heard a visiting minister speak at her church, dreamed that she was attracted to the preacher and that she was in bed with him.

As you can imagine the dream was quite distressing to her. However, what she was attracted to was the dynamic gift of God that was very evident in his life. The dream was a reflection of her wanting the type of intimacy that this man had with God.

Recently, when in Europe, I sat with a young couple to help them through some difficulties in their marriage. They were a good-looking couple. He was concerned that she was infatuated and attracted to their Youth Pastor. The husband said it was all to do with a series of dreams she'd had in which she found herself attracted to their youth minister.

In one of her dreams, she had been sitting down and talking to the Youth Pastor while her husband was in another room, watching passively and showing little interest.

After questioning her husband it became apparent that his Christian walk was luke-warm, just as it was reflected in his wife's dream of him being passive. She told me how unhappy she had been with his sluggish attitude toward spiritual matters. However, she'd misunderstood the dream, taking it as literal instead of metaphorical. It really reflected the frustration she felt with her husband's lack of spiritual strength and leadership. Her dreams, much like those in the previous example, had more to do with her desire for the type of spiritual strength that the youth minister possessed.

RAPE

At the conclusion of a seminar a woman and her husband approached me to ask about a series of recurring nightmares. She would find herself in several dreams being raped by a stranger. She was afraid that her husband would leave her.

Often in a case like this, there has been abuse of some kind, physical or verbal. In this case it proved to be a violation of her physical life; tragically someone had abused her sexually and taken away her dignity and self worth. This had obviously taken its toll on their marriage. The husband was faithfully and lovingly committed to her. Though her dream was highlighting an area of uncertainty, thinking that her husband might want to leave her in real life. It was wonderful to see her husband reaffirming his love for her.

When someone has suffered in this way from past abuses, until they have come to a point of total healing, there is a strong possibility that such dreams may recur.

DREAM THEME 9: TOILET

The first question that may be asked is, what is it that has made its way into your system (life) that you need to eliminate or dispose of. Perhaps it's pain from the past, some hurt that you have carried.

When conducting seminars this symbol is frequently asked about.

DOES ANYBODY CARE

Recently at a seminar a quietly spoken woman approached me about a dream in which she was searching for a toilet. She said there was one toilet six feet high in the air that was out of reach. There was another one on the floor that was crowded by people who were talking around it, with no regard for her need. She felt too embarrassed to ask them to move and remembered feeling frustrated and let down by them.

I asked her if she wanted to unload certain cares that she has been carrying. A toilet out of reach above could suggest that she felt as though she wasn't making a connection with God. Perhaps she didn't feel that God would care too much about her struggles.

I reminded her of the Scripture in 1 Peter 5:7, *"Cast all your anxiety on Him because He cares for you."*

The other toilet that was crowded by people who gave no regard to her need reflected something else. Not only did she believe the Lord couldn't help her, she was convinced that people didn't care for her either. The dream seemed to be instructing her to be more open and willing to share her struggles, both with God and people.

Restrooms are a clear symbol of a place we visit to eliminate unwanted matter. The very name 'restroom' is symbolic of a place of rest and relief. It can represent a place where you can rid yourself of old habit patterns, weights, concerns, fears, failures and insecurities.

In the same way that your physical body cannot survive in good health without proper elimination, so the emotional and spiritual side of your life must dispose of its unwanted hindrances. The writer of the book of Hebrews puts it like this,

"...let us throw off everything that hinders and the sin that so easily entangles, and let us run with perseverance the race marked out for us..." Hebrews 12:1-2

CHAPTER 8

Are recurring dreams important?

"Both dreams mean the same thing,"Joseph told Pharaoh."God was telling you what He is going to do here in the land of Egypt."
Genesis 41:25 The Living Bible

RECURRING DREAMS

It is said that Ronald Reagan had repeated dreams of a White House. Thereupon the realtor showed him a big white house with bay windows that he felt he could not afford. After Reagan became President and was in the real White House, he never had that dream again.[1]

I remember when I was a child, at times when I was thoroughly occupied with an activity, my mother would often have to repeat herself. When she would call me for dinner, for instance, it would often have to be more than once and with an increase in volume each time she repeated it. She would have to repeat this until she was able to interrupt what I was doing and obtain my undivided attention. Doesn't say much for my attention span, does it?

Repetitive dreams are rather like this. If there is an important message that needs to be communicated, the dream simply persists until the individual has responded in the appropriate way. Recurring dreams that are ignored long enough may return as nightmares.

Sometimes a repetitive dream will stop without any apparent reason. This could be because we've made the required changes without necessarily thinking about them. Perhaps we've resolved our circumstances by changing jobs, taking a new attitude towards life and people, or establishing peace in a troubled relationship.

Consider the following example

Recently I spoke to a friend whom I had not seen for some twenty-five years. Both our families had been relatively close during my early years. We talked a little of the old days and where we each were now. After telling her that I was working on this book, she told me that ever since she was 5 or 6 years of age, for 30 years, she had had the same dream over and over again. I asked her to describe it to me.

Her dream had always been of a dark figure next to her, which had made her fearful and afraid.

I asked her what or who she felt the figure represented. She said she knew the dark figure stood for her father. Her dad had left the family when she was very young. He hadn't been the kindest of fathers. Thirty years later she moved interstate in search of her father. She finally found him and tried all she could to rebuild a relationship, but with little success. It was interesting to note that since confronting her father the dream had ceased.

Some of our dreams reflect certain fears that we have, which, when confronted during the day, cease to appear during the night. A powerful lesson can be learnt from my friend's dream: that we must confront our fears. Many of us shy away from coming face-to-face with the things we fear.

Michael Pritchard said it well: "Fear is that darkroom where negatives are developed." For those of us who know anything of photography, we know that once the negatives are exposed to light the image is gone. Notice how her dream (image) ceased once she confronted her fear.

RECURRING DREAMS CAN HAVE DIFFERENT IMAGES AND SYMBOLS WHILE CARRYING THE SAME MESSAGE

Consider Pharaoh's dream in Genesis 41:1-7

1st DREAM: He dreamt of seven cows, sleek and fat. They grazed among the reeds. Then seven other cows, ugly and gaunt, came up out of the Nile and stood beside those on the riverbank. The cows that were ugly and gaunt ate the seven sleek and fat cows. Then Pharaoh woke up.

2nd DREAM: He fell asleep again and had a second dream. *Seven* heads of grain healthy and good were growing on a single stalk. After them *seven* other heads of grain sprouted, thin and scorched by the east wind. The thin heads of grain swallowed up the *seven* healthy full heads. When Pharaoh woke up he realised it had been a dream.

When Joseph was called upon to solve the mystery his reply was similar to Daniel's.

In verse 16 "I cannot do it," Joseph replied to Pharaoh, "but God will give Pharaoh the answer he desires." He says the same thing in Genesis 40:8 to the chief cupbearer and the chief baker: "Do not interpretations belong to God?"

We must continue to remind ourselves that God alone knows all things and is able to help us with the required insight and revelation into the world of dreams and visions. Let us be careful to give Him all glory and all honour.

Joseph proceeded to tell Pharaoh the interpretation while making it very clear that God had shown him so.

In verse 25: "Then Joseph said to Pharaoh the dreams are *one and the same...*" In both cases the dream contained exactly the same message though presented differently. It is interesting to note how the theme of 'seven' runs through both of them.

I've found that a recurring dream is nearly always delivering a strong and firm message.

"The reason the dream was given to Pharaoh in *two forms* is that the matter has been *firmly* decided by God and God will do it soon." Genesis 41:32

In other words a recurring dream could very well be trying to emphasize a very important message.

PUNNY THINGS IN DREAMS

According to the Grosset Webster dictionary the word 'pun' stands for: a play on words, which are similar in sound but different in meaning.[2]

An example of a pun is reflected in the story of a Chinese scholar who was lecturing when all the lights went out. He asked the members of the audience to raise their hands. As soon as they had all complied, the lights went on again. He then said, "Prove wisdom of old Chinese saying: *Many hands make light work.*"

Consider some of the following examples as puns:

Sick in the gut: A deep-seated issue or point of upset.

A dream of a bare chest: getting something off one's chest.

A man shooting me down: a fear of being attacked verbally.

A bulldozer: assertive behaviour.

Losing face: embarrassment.

Spineless: lacking stamina and substance.

An ear to the ground: attentiveness and alertness.

Hard-nosed: stubbornness inflexibility, insensitivity.

Two-faced: untruthful, saying one thing but doing another.

Butterflies in the stomach: nervousness.[3]

My wife had a funny dream which the interpretation came through understanding of pun.

A FISH OUT OF WATER

Not long after we had moved to a new church in a new town to take up the position as associate pastor, my wife had a strange dream about fish.

She dreamed of a fish bowl with two goldfish swimming around in it. Then she saw another goldfish floating around the room. She saw herself trying to catch the floating fish, and eventually succeeded, putting it back in the fish bowl with the other two fish.

To understand the dream, of course, we considered our current situation. Being in a new community, Kate couldn't help but feel a little out of it. There were two other pastor's wives in this new church, and being the new kid on the block, she had compared herself with them, and felt inadequate.

When she told me about the dream I couldn't help but laugh as I said, "You're feeling so out of it that you feel like a fish out of water." The Lord was using the dream to tell her that she was just as valuable as the others working in the new church, and that she did belong in the same environment (bowl) with them.

CHAPTER 9

Nightmares

*"I had a dream that made me afraid.
AS I was lying in my bed, the images and visions t
hat passed through my mind terrified me."*

King Nebuchadnezzar, Daniel 4:5

NIGHTMARES

Many dreams are unpleasant, even terrifying, as in the case of nightmares. They can be among the most disturbing of all human experiences. Consider dream situations where the dreamer is being chased by a man with a knife, or when he finds himself drowning and gasping for air; when she shoots her mother at point blank range; when a burglar enters the room; a lion is about to spring on him; someone has pushed her out of the aircraft and she had no parachute; the house is on fire; he is arrested and put into prison and only fears the worst.

Some people refer to nightmares as punishment dreams. Others say a nightmare is the price you pay for doing wrong, rebelling against authority, a forbidden indulgence, for having committed some offence, or even having yielded to a temptation.

While this may or may not be the case, some nightmares can be the result of stressful situations, worry and anxiety. Situations such as job loss, parenthood, divorce, and change of lifestyle can be sufficient to trigger a nightmare.

A child may experience a nightmare after discipline has been administered, when he/she is sick, during the tumult surrounding a divorce or moving from one location to another. The older the child the more the nightmare could be a reflection of some anxiety or fear they are facing through school or life in general. A nightmare may also be encouraging you to confront certain fears that you have been unwilling to face up to.

Nightmares usually occur towards the end of a long REM period in the latter half of the night, almost as though the dream were building to its climax of terror. Generally speaking the more alarming the nightmare the more severe the message. Where some dreams can be like an alarm clock going off, the severe nightmare is more like a city siren.

Author Valerie Moolman, consultant to the Serta Sleep Centre, has this to say on the topic of nightmares: "Nightmares are the most common of dream disturbances; we all have them at some time or another. One major study showed that, in young adults, two out of five dreams can be expected to contain sequences of fear; and another reported that two out of three dreams tend to be unpleasant. This should be easy enough to understand if we accept the proposition that one of the major reasons for dreaming is to work out our conflicts."[1]

Perhaps the writer of Job puts it into reality for us: "When I think my bed will comfort me and my couch will ease my complaint, even then you frighten me with dreams and terrify me with visions..." Job 7: 13-14

There are occasions when God will allow a nightmare to bring to someone's attention a matter that they are ignoring. A dream can become a nightmare, especially when the dreamer gives little or no consideration to his or her ways.

King Nebuchadnezzar, in his arrogance, refused to heed his dreams and they turned into nightmares. A nightmare is a dream bad enough to awaken us in anxiety, its haunting imagery lingering sometimes for days.

If a nightmare's origin is from God, His motivation in every instance is to direct the person's life back to the right path. It could be said that it literally 'frightens the hell out of them'. Once again our reference from Job shows that God can use moments like these to steer man away from danger and personal harm.

"In a dream, in a vision of the night, when deep sleep falls on men as they slumber in their beds, He may speak in their ears and *terrify them* with warnings, to turn man from wrongdoing and keep him from pride, to preserve his soul from the pit, his life from perishing by the sword." Job 33:15-18

DREAM OF HORROR

Though I can't go into details of this example, I have sat with one young man and listened to an account of his horrific nightmare. The violent and gruesome dream revealed some very troubling things; things that I had already suspected about the boy. But even when I spoke to him about it, he was quite adamant that he wasn't going to change, and that he had in fact taken to reading the satanic bible. I was very disappointed, particularly because I knew what that meant for him. Some time later though, it was revealed that all was not lost. I had been preaching about the Power of God, and His desire that people should be free from the darkness of stubbornness and rebellion. When I asked for people to respond for prayer, this young man came to the front to be prayed for. He'd come to the point where he wanted to be free from the dark and evil things that had previously gripped his life.

After the service, he spoke to me and told me how he had planned to get a gun and shoot the youth pastor in that church. At that point I began to thank God again that he'd been set free.

Not all nightmares have to revolve around the theme of outright evil. It is important to look at what appropriate action is required in order to respond to the message given by the dream.[2]

Take the following case, where a young lady came to me with a dream. To interpret this one I asked the people who were at one of my seminars to help me by using the five laws. I was very impressed with their insight.

The following dream caused a lot of emotional distress to the dreamer. Only young and newly married, she was frustrated with her husband who played the passive leader in their home. In total contrast to him she's always been a very motivated person both at home and in her leadership role at church.

TEARING ME APART

She dreamed her husband was fishing in a hole. He caught a big fish but couldn't pull it up. The perspective of the dream changed to a horizontal tunnel, where there was a light coming towards them. The husband was tearing the flesh off dead people and using it for bait. He ran out of dead people and started killing others.

He hung a lady upside down and began to skin her. The dreamer was screaming watching her husband eating the people like a sandwich. She felt really sick and as though she couldn't handle it. She put the bodies in the boot of the car noticing the dead smell. She drove around trying to find a place to dump the bodies, not wanting anybody to find out. She felt anxious that she would get caught.

I had to wonder how such a violent dream could make its way into a person's nightlife without the person's permission. It was enormously disturbing, but the interpretation that the seminar class came up with proved to be very helpful.

D – DETERMINE whether the dream is literal or metaphorical. In this case the dream was symbolic.

R – RECENT CONCERNS: I asked her about the direction of her life. She openly shared her frustration about her husband's passivity, and how at times she literally cried in desperation, hoping that things would change.

E – EVALUATE the moods and emotions of the dream (feeling tone). It was very obvious that the nightmare was distressing to her.

A – ASK God to reveal what the symbolism stands for.
I encouraged the whole class to pray and ask the Holy Spirit for revelation concerning this dream, making them understand that this dream was really important to the young lady.

M – MAKE sure the interpretation rings true with the dreamer. They and only they will know if it's right for them.

As it was, she agreed with the interpretation remarking on how helpful and releasing it had been for her.

She'd dreamt her husband was fishing in a hole, and he caught a big fish but couldn't pull it up: *She had put too high an expectation on him; he was trying to please her by matching up to her expectations of him. But he couldn't pull the fish up.*

The perspective of the dream changed to that of a horizontal tunnel with a light coming towards them: *Perspective was the key word. She needed to change her perspective and understand that there was a light at the end of the tunnel.*

He was tearing off the flesh from dead people and using it for bait. When he'd run out of dead people he'd started killing others. He hung a lady upside down and begun to skin her: *There was a lot of flesh in this scene. The Bible speaks of the flesh as the wrong way of going about things.*

She had run out of fleshly (her own) means and ways of dealing with this. This whole situation had turned her life upside down. Skin can represent covering and security, and in her dream the body is skinned, an indication of where she had actually found herself; totally insecure and unprotected.

She was screaming. Her husband was eating the people like a sandwich, which made her feel really sick: *Her emotions are screaming out while she feels sandwiched in the ordeal with no way out. The whole experience is now not just sickening and hard to live with on the outside, it is now swallowed and eating her up on the inside. She is deeply disturbed by it.*

She could not handle it, and puts the bodies in the boot of her car. She remembers the dead smell. She drove around looking for a place to dump them, all the while feeling anxious that she would get caught:
She can't handle it, and has stowed all of her failed approaches with her husband in the back of the car. The situation in her marriage has started to decay and she hasn't wanted anybody to know what's been going on. (I was the only person she'd spoken to about the situation. The class didn't know her identity)

She felt anxious lest anyone should find out about her marriage and its rocky situation. The dream theme title was very appropriate to this situation: IT'S JUST TEARING ME APART.

She had become so obsessed with wanting her husband to become someone he wasn't, that it was eating her up on the inside and robbing her of the joy in her marriage.

CAN NIGHTMARES BE DEALT WITH NEVER TO RETURN?

Yes! Absolutely. For many of my teenage years I lived in fear of the dark and had demonic interruptions to my sleep. When I became a Christian, I began to read the Bible and came across a passage of Scripture that helped me find release from fears and nightmares.

"When you lie down you will not be afraid; when you lie down your sleep will be sweet." Proverbs 3:24.

Another reference from the book of Psalms reinforces the Lord's protection on our lives:

"I will lie down and sleep in peace, for you alone O Lord, make me dwell in safety." Psalm 4:8

I have often prayed with people who've struggled with night time fears, and after having shown them these Scriptures, they have reported how they don't have trouble sleeping any more.

The Bible teaches, His Holy Word is a lamp, and a light. Psalm 119:105.

When I thought about this, I came to the conclusion that the penetrating and piercing light of His Word can and does extinguish every fearful and darkened corridor in my life.

Not every nightmare contains a message. Some people have nightmares because of the things they have seen or heard. They might have exposed their minds to certain horror movies, books, occult practices etc. These are the sorts of things that foster a spirit of fear in a person's life.

Before my family became Christians, my mother used to tell me occult stories, sometimes in a graphic way. At that time she didn't know the effect that it could and did have on her young children, and she is not unlike many parents today. They allow their children to watch television and movies that expose them to what they think is harmless, mild horror and occult. Many people think it is just make-believe and fantasy.

When my oldest daughter was very young she often woke in fright after a nightmare. Of my three children, she was the most timid while growing up. Both Kate and I would read Scriptures to her and pray over her every night but nothing changed. Then Kate had an idea to place a CD player in her bedroom and play some worship music while she was going to sleep. She has never had a problem with nightmares since.

We can never underestimate the power in worship. A young woman told me of a time at a friend's birthday party when a few of her friends were playing the ouija board (a board used to conjure up spirits into the room). The girls would ask the spirit a question and the demonic power would communicate to them by moving an object to different letters set around the board.

As a Christian, this girl knew how dangerous this activity was, so, not wanting to cause a scene, she simply asked if she could play the piano over in the corner. She sat down and began to play a church chorus, 'The power of His love', and the whole atmosphere of the room changed. Whatever spirit had been manipulating the board stopped and the girls playing the board turned to her and shouted, "Hey! What are you doing, you messed the whole show up."

I was so pleased to hear what had happened, to realise that this girl's choice to worship God had filled the room with the light of God's presence and there was no place left for darkness.

CHAPTER 10

Supernatural dreams and visions

"From the beginning, the two primary ways the Lord has spoken to His people have been through dreams and visions. However this is probably the least understood subject in the church."[1]

Rick Joyner

SUPERNATURAL DREAMS & VISIONS

What is a supernatural dream? I believe the messages contained in these sorts of dreams are divinely sent. They can be glimpses into the future, a revelation or insight for your own life, family, church, city, nation or the nations.

Supernatural dreams and visions can be prophetic in nature, confirming God's given assignment and call for your life. Personally I have not found these dreams to be a regular occurrence, however, they are quite obvious when they do occur. Such dreams are mostly answers to matters of prayer, and direction in major decisions.

A young woman I know who has a Doctorate in Microbiology told me that in her second year of university she was struggling to balance certain mathematical figures to a statistics assignment that was due. That night she dreamt a series of figures, which turned out to be the correct answer she was looking for.

I have often said to this young lady that I believe the Lord can unfold and unlock the secrets for cures to deadly diseases, lethal viruses and the common cold if only we would pray and ask Him to show us.

If one can dream the answer to a mathematical equation, who knows if another night you might wake up with a ground-breaking scientific discovery.

SIX BEAUTIFUL ROSES

Good Morning Holy Spirit is a book written by Benny Hinn. In it he records a dream that his mother once had. She dreamt she saw six beautiful roses in her hand. Jesus entered the room; He came to her and asked her for one. She willingly gave Him one of the roses. As the dream continued, a short slim young man with dark hair came over to her and wrapped her in a warm cloth.

The very next day, December 3rd, 1952, Benny Hinn was born. The Hinn family was eventually to have six boys and two girls. She later told Benny that he was the rose that she presented to Jesus. What an incredible global impact this 'rose' is having in the world.[2]

THE NIGHT I MET SMITH WIGGLESWORTH

Smith Wigglesworth opened the front door to my house and walked into the living room. I was completely surprised and overwhelmed by this dynamic and respected evangelist coming to visit. I watched as he went to the bathroom to freshen up, (symbolic of stirring afresh the gift of God). By this point in the dream I was so overwhelmed that I couldn't stop weeping. I felt the intense power of God in my dream. As Smith Wigglesworth walked back into the room, I was trying to hold back the tears, leaning against the chair and holding on. This great man of God, who is called the Apostle of Faith, was known as a radical healing evangelist of his day. In my dream he was wearing his normal three-piece suit and was well groomed. As he looked at me with loving, strong and steely eyes he said: "You want to go higher, don't you?" I replied, "Yes! I want to cast my seed on green fields." (Symbolic of sowing my life and time into rich fertile soil - places where people are hungry to hear and know His truth). Looking at me he pointed his finger towards me and said, "What is needed in the day that you live is the word of knowledge."

The dream occurred during a time when I had committed myself to prayer and a fast. I had an incredible desire to see extraordinary, even peculiar moves of God. I began to think of what this great man had said in my dream: "What is needed in the day that you live is the word of knowledge." I began to ask myself why this healing evangelist, who would pray for people and see cancers disappear, who would in boldness tear growths off someone's body and they would be instantly healed, would seem to place a greater importance on the word of knowledge for the day in which I lived. He did not insinuate that any one gift of The Holy Spirit was more important than the other; however I understood the word of knowledge to be clearly more influential for my day. (The nine gifts of the Spirit are recorded in 1 Corinthians 12:7-10)

The more I thought about it the more I could see how the message was true. We are living in a day of reason and technological advances like no other time in history. With the advancement of modern medicine and the ability to explain mind over matter, mankind has become cynical and self sufficient; curing his own diseases, and able to perform medical feats that are extraordinary: Feats such as open-heart surgery, chemotherapy, body part replacements, cloning and so on. In our day of logic and rationalism, people are quick to explain a miraculous healing as mind over matter, self-belief, etc. However when you operate in the word of knowledge and begin to reveal events and facts about a person's life, of which you previously knew nothing except by divine insight, people are left dumbfounded and perplexed. They ask questions like: "How did you know that?"; "Who told you?"; "Where did you find that information from?"; "I never mentioned this to anybody." In this matter the message that God was telling me through the symbol of Smith Wiggelsworth was right. People are unable to dispute divine revelation.

THE DAY I MET MY MATCH

Some years ago, I went with a team of young people to do street outreach during the Americas Cup in Perth. The method we used at the time was street drama, followed by the members of the drama team intermingling with the crowd and talking to different individuals about the message of the drama. I had drawn the short straw and been cast in the part of the devil, and therefore was dressed accordingly, in red and black, with my face painted to look like something out of the Rocky Horror Show. When the drama finished I made my way toward what seemed to me like a gang of young men. I had this wild idea to see if I could make an impression on the leader of the gang. You might say it was the day I met my match.

The young fellow was not very talkative; nevertheless I worked hard trying to stimulate conversation about the drama. Suddenly he stopped me in my tracks by placing his face right up to mine, and with an agitated look of defiance said, "If you keep talking to me about this Jesus stuff, I'll kill you man."

There was an air of seriousness in his comment, and I suddenly felt the urge to summon support from the others in the team. With the same amount of urgency, they seemed to be trying to keep as far as possible away from me and the scene I was causing. That they were busily praying for me, so they told me later, wasn't really of much encouragement at the time.

I didn't quite know how to respond to this threat. All I could think of was the line David Wilkinson, the country preacher, used, when confronted with the same threat from Nicki Cruz, the New York gang leader. David had bravely said, "You could cut me up into a thousand pieces and scatter them all across the pavement and each one of those pieces would still be looking at you and saying, Jesus loves you man."

What inspiration! "Grant," I said, "you could cut me up into a thousand pieces and scatter them all over the pavement and each piece would be looking at you saying, 'Jesus loves you.'"

It was brilliantly delivered, as though I had rehearsed it a hundred times. The only problem was it didn't work. Grant was angrier than before and this time with fire in his eyes, he put his nose up to mine and told me he was carrying a knife and would have no trouble using it on me. It would be an understatement to say I began to feel rather awkward.

I have always disliked coming out second best, though I was not sure what to do. I contemplated whether I should just leave, or give it one more go. *Zoran! What on earth has got into you?* Beneath my breath I silently prayed and asked The Holy Spirit to show me something of his life. I was getting quite desperate by now.

But God answered my rather nervous prayer and I began to see something and spoke out what the Holy Spirit was saying to me. "Correct me if I am wrong," I said, and was sure he would. "I want to tell you something about yourself. You are living with your dad, however, the problem is, your mother has left your father and you don't get on with the other woman who has moved into your house. This troubles you greatly and you wish that things could be as they were. You are angry with your dad and blame him for your mother walking out. Deep down inside you is a boy crying out for help. Am I right or wrong?"

He looked at me with tears beginning to form and in a vocabulary not fit for a dictionary basically said, "how did you #!%^# know? Who told you all that?" I gently told him of God's deep love for him, and how much he wanted to touch his life. Embarrassed by his apparent display of emotional weakness, he ran off down the street. This left his companions standing with this weird guy who is dressed in red and black looking like the devil. I turned to the remaining lads and said, "Now then boys. Who's next?" That was the quickest crowd dispersion I've ever seen.

However, it didn't end there. Later Grant came into the coffee shop our group were running, and began to talk to some of our Christian workers. I will never know what happened to that young man. Nor will I ever forget the day the word of knowledge was activated in my life and how the Holy Spirit drew back the curtain on Grant's home life.

CAN GOD SPEAK TO CHILDREN IN DREAMS AND VISIONS?

Often young minds can be more receptive than older ones. Scripture teaches us that God *can* speak to children. "Your sons and daughters will prophesy, your young men will see visions..." Acts 2:17. We see in another instance, 1Samuel 3, where God speaks to Samuel as a boy, though at first he doesn't recognise it is the Lord.

When my oldest daughter was about seven years old, I asked her to close her eyes, and then told her that I was going to pray and ask the Holy Spirit to give her a vision to show her about her life now. Not knowing what to expect, but trusting her dad, she willingly complied. After praying for her I asked whether she saw something. She answered, "Dad, I see a small tree with two apples on it."

She didn't know what it meant, I quickly explained what the Lord had shown her was her life; that at this time she was a little girl (small tree), who has begun bearing fruit in her Christian walk (referring to

John 15 and the four levels of fruitfulness - no fruit, fruit, more fruit and much fruit.)

My younger daughter was watching us and asked, "Hey dad! Can I play that game too?"

I was reminded of the time God asked the young prophet Jeremiah to do the same exercise. The story is recorded in the Bible Jeremiah 1:11.

'The Word of the Lord came to me: "What do you see, Jeremiah?"

"I see the branch of an almond tree," I replied.

The Lord said to me, "You have seen correctly, for I am watching to see that my word is fulfilled."'

What significance does the branch of an almond tree hold in relation to Jeremiah's call as a prophet? The Hebrew word for almond is *shaqued* (pronounced 'shaw-kade'), which describes the almond tree when it is in early bloom. So here we have the budding of a young prophet who has just started out in service. He receives the assurance of God's faithfulness as He watches over the completion of His word on Jeremiah's life.[3]

Considering the Biblical examples of Samuel and Jeremiah, I think it is safe to assume that God can and does speak to young children in dreams and visions.

THE END OF THE WORLD

My wife came to me one morning and told me of an incredible dream she'd had.

I dreamt I was at the local cemetery and I saw human spirits ascending out of their graves and rising into the sky. As they rose I heard a voice say, "The dead in Christ shall rise first and after that the rest will follow.

Both my wife and I were convinced that she'd received a first-hand glimpse into a future event that is recorded in 1 Thessalonians 4:16-18.

144 | IN YOUR DREAMS

I seem to be coming across an increasing number of people who have dreamed about events pertaining to the end of the world. Some of these dreams have contained images of a nuclear holocaust, others of global famine. Not long after the World Trade Centre devastation a friend of mine dreamt the world was being wrapped up like a ball of wool and it wasn't long before the light went out.

It is quite possible that such dreams are snap shots of events to come. Perhaps the most common of all has been numerous accounts of people who have dreamt about the return of Jesus Christ as has been prophesied in the Bible.

In the years following 9/11the whole world has experienced a heightened awareness of the global phenomenon called global terror. Religious extremists have taken it upon themselves to threaten Western countries and infidels with the fear of death by terror attack. While we have seen and heard of many such attacks right across the world, God still seems to be at work, even in those countries where extreme religious ideals exist. There have been numerous reports of Muslim people, even religious leaders of Islam, experiencing dreams that have led them to salvation through Jesus Christ. The dreams have been so powerful, that there have been a number of people who have converted to Christianity even under the threat of persecution and death.

One such case, reported to the Open Doors USA group in 2015, was the story of a young man who had been trained in an Islamic school to be an imam. He had been serving Islam with a zeal for many years when he suddenly encountered Jesus Christ in a dream.

"There was an incident in 2002 where I had a vision from the Lord early in the morning around 3 a.m.," he said. "In the vision, I saw Jesus very clearly telling me to follow Him."

"My wife asked me what happened in my dream, because I woke up very startled, and when I explained it to her, she was scared and said,

'We are going to be infidels, so we need to pray.'" He told her which Quranic verses Jesus told him to read in his dream, and that each verse specifically instructs the reader to follow and believe in Jesus.

When he returned to sleep, [he] immediately had another vision of Jesus. "Jesus appeared saying 'It's Me, follow Me. When you follow Me you will pay a price, there will be persecution in your life, but in the end, you will be victorious. I am with you.'" [4]

Because of the fierce ideology within some of the extreme religious groups, it is dangerous for converts to Christianity to make their new found faith too public, however the testimonies are filtering through various missionary organisations. One of the common elements in these testimonies is how Jesus has come in a dream and bid the dreamer to follow Him to salvation.

HOW WILL YOUR LIFE END?

Whatever your view on how this world will finish up, one thing is for certain, finish it will. The hourglass is fast running out of sand and our time coming to a close. The Bible has clearly prophesied and predicted it:

"Then I saw a new heaven and a new earth, for the first heaven and the first earth had passed away..." (Revelation 21:1)

September 11, 2001 will be remembered as one of the most tragic events ever to take place on our planet. The terrorist attack on The World Trade Centre in New York City has, like never before, brought an air of global uncertainty to international security. Never have the words of Jesus sounded louder or more clear than for this time. When asked by His disciples in Matthew 24, "What will be the sign of your coming and the end of the age?" Jesus answered, "...You will hear of wars and rumours of wars, but see to it that you are not alarmed. Such things must happen, but the end is still to come. Nation will rise against nation and kingdom against kingdom. There will be famines and earthquakes in various places. All these are but the beginning." Jesus went on to say that in these closing days, "...because of an increase of wickedness, the love of most will grow cold, but he who stands firm to the end will be saved."

There are so many options being offered as the hunger for peace of mind increases: horoscopes, mystics, psychics etc. There is transcendentalism, pantheism, materialism, reincarnation, liberalism, atheism etc. But in my wide experience of helping people, only a relationship with the Lord Jesus Christ has ever met the deepest need and answered the hardest question.

Perhaps your coming across this book is no coincidence, as I believe the Lord Jesus Christ would like to present you with an opportunity to make your peace with Him. It is a chance to ask Him to live in your life. It is more than just an assurance of eternal life. You will also discover there is a purpose and destiny in this life; that you are not just an accident or mistake, but God has created you for a great purpose. You will know the Lord's peace that goes way beyond all understanding, and in the middle of chaos and trouble you will know calm. God wants to give faith instead of fear, and light in time of darkness.

Now is as good a time as any. Even as you read this, you can pray this prayer:

"Father God,

I thank you for your love and grace, and I acknowledge the finished work of your Son Jesus Christ, on the cross.

I recognize that Jesus died for me, and took upon Himself my sins, and that He rose from the dead in order to make a way back to you, my Heavenly Father.

I confess with my mouth, that you are Lord.
With my heart I believe that I am cleansed from my sin, and
am now saved.
Help me Lord, to live the life you want me to live.
In the name of Jesus Christ, and by the power of the Holy
Spirit.
Amen"

If you have prayed this prayer for the first time, may I be the
first to congratulate you on the best decision that you will ever make
in your life. May The Lord bless you, guide you and keep His hand
upon your life. If you don't have a Bible, be sure to purchase one and
start reading one of the Gospels, Matthew, Mark, Luke or John. Find
yourself a good church, and let them know that you have prayed and
asked Christ into your life.

CONCLUSION

As we come to the end of this discussion on dreams I'd like to leave you with some important principles you should consider when interpreting your dreams. The word PRINCIPLES is used as an acronym to break down ten points you can use as a guide to what you should and shouldn't do.

TEN PATTERNS AND PRINCIPLES

P   Peruse the Word of the Lord and come to know Him. "The secret of the Lord is with them that fear Him; and He will show them His covenant." Psalm 25:14 KJV
Understanding the Scripture will further enhance your knowledge of symbols.

R   Remember that most dreams are subjective, meaning they apply to you only. Be very careful about trying to convince someone else that the dream is about them.

I   Investigate and research the subject of dreams. For further material refer to the bibliography at the back of the book. Beware that much of what is available in various libraries and bookshops will not line up with the Bible. If in doubt consult your minister who is skilled in understanding the Word of the Lord.

N   Never take the validity of your own interpretation for granted. Should you try and interpret someone else's dream, be sure to leave the meaning up to the dreamer. Make certain that your interpretation does not contradict Scripture.

C   Care should be taken not to rely on dreams as your one and only source of direction for life. God can choose to speak to you in a multitude of different ways. "For God does speak – now one way, now another…" Job 33:14

I   Interpreting other people's dreams should be avoided until you are confident with interpreting your own.

P   Pen and paper. Ensure that you have these items by your bedside so that you may record your dreams. Remember, the Bible would never have been written unless it was for those who kept diligent record. "Daniel had a dream, and visions passed through his mind as he was lying on his bed. He *wrote down* the substance of his dream." Daniel 7:1. This is also saying to God that you are in a place of readiness at all times.

L   Leave no room for procrastination - 'I'll do it later'. Write it down immediately as the chances are you will not remember it in the morning.

E   Easy does it! You don't have to strive to interpret dreams. You may not understand all that you dream. The Lord is able to speak to you through other means as well.

S   Seek counsel from a sensible well-balanced person. If you have dreamed about another person, be wise and sensitive in your approach to them.

I hope that you have been enriched and encouraged by the material presented. Most of all I pray that this book has aroused a hunger and thirst in you to seek the Maker of heaven and earth. It is God our Heavenly Father who holds the blueprint to the purpose and plan for your life. If you seek Him you will find Him.

'IN YOUR DREAMS'

The colours of the sky radiate,
as the sun slips silently away,
and as the moon and the stars glisten in its place,
all is calm, is quiet.
Gone are the tempests of the day,
So sleep my weary one,
rest your head,
take no troubled thoughts to your bed.
But rather dream of Kings and Queens
or of flying high, or mountain scenes.
For *in your dreams*
you can conquer all,
So sleep my friend,
Sleep one and all.

Kate Paunovich

END NOTES & BIBLIOGRAPHY

Introduction

1   Rick Joyner, *A Prophetic Vision for the 21st Century*, Thomas Nelson Publishers Inc, Nashville, Tennessee. 1999, Chapter 6, Page 86. Excerpts used by permission Morning Star Fellowship Church, website: www.morningstarministries.org

2   Wilda. B. Tanner, *The Mystical and Magical Marvellous World of Dreams*, Published in USA by Sparrow Hawk Press, Tahlequah, Oklahoma. 1988 Page 10.

Chapter 1

1   Herman H. Riffel, *Dreams: Giants and Geniuses in the Making*, 1996. Page 3-4. Destiny Image Publishers, 167 Walnut Bottom Road, Shippensburg, PA 17257. www.destinyimage.com

2   A. F. Ferguson Stewart, *Australia's Grace Darling*, Printed by Rob Griffiths, Printer Busselton, WA and Published by the Augusta – Margaret River Tourist Bureau (Inc) 1946, Page 2 – 3.

3   Illustrated Sydney News 3/2/ 1877, National Library of Australia

4   Paul Lee Tan, ed., *Encyclopaedia of 7700 Illustrations* (Rockville, Md.: Assurance Publishers, 1979), article 4775.

5   Herman H. Riffel, Dreams: *Giants and Geniuses in the Making*, 1996. Page 2 Destiny Image Publishers. 167 Walnut Bottom Road, Shippensburg, PA 17257. www.destinyimage.com

6   Ann Spangler. Dreams: *Miracles Can Happen in the Middle of the Night*. Grand Rapids, Michigan. Zondervan Publishing House. 1997. Page 92.

7   R. A. Brown and R. G. Lucknock, *Dreams, Daydreams and Discovery*, A paper for the Polytechnic of North London, Holloway, London, England.

8   Ann Spangler. *Dreams: Miracles Can Happen in the Middle of the Night*. Grand Rapids, Michigan. Zondervan Publishing House. 1997. Page 93.

9   Wilda B. Tanner, *The Mystical and Magical Marvellous World of Dreams*, Published in USA by Sparrow Hawk Press, Tahlequah, Oklahoma, 1988. Page 1.

10 Ann Spangler. Dreams: *Miracles Can Happen in the Middle of the Night*. Grand Rapids, Michigan. Zondervan Publishing House. 1997. Page 93.

‾ and Geniuses in the Making, 1996. Page 33.
167 Walnut Bottom Road, Shippensburg, PA

⌐Macaughly, Discovery Psychology Video 13,
,go, Victoria, Australia.
. A Way to Listen to God, 1989, Page 34. Publisher
w York/Mahwah, N.J. Used with permission of Paulist
,ress.com
, God, Dreams and Revelation. (Minneapolis.:, MiAm:
ess Publishers. 1991), Page. 17.
,r book of Morton T. Kelsey's is as thorough as they come on the
,ams. In it he gives an overview of the history of the interpretation
ა, the author traces the development of Judeo Christian attitudes
,reams from Old and New Testament times, through the period of
,ntenment, to the present. He also covers the attitudes and convictions of
, early church fathers on the subject.
,verett Ferguson, ed. Encyclopaedia of Early Christianity, Garland Publishers
Inc. 1992 Page 280 – 281.
ა John A. Sanford, Dreams: God's Forgotten Language. San Francisco: Harper &
Row, 1988
17 Morton Kelsey, Dreams: A Way to Listen to God, Publisher Paulist Press USA,
1989, Page 77,74.
Used with permission of Paulist Press. www.paulistpress.com
An excellent and very readable summary on the subject of REM was written by
Jill Neimark in the Psychology Today Magazine July/August 1998 Edition. A
more comprehensive and visual account of the dreaming mind was compiled by
Hobson and Macaughly, Discovery Psychology Video 13, LaTrobe University,
Bendigo, Victoria, Australia. A detailed survey of the material on experimental
study of sleep was compiled by Charles Fisher in his article "Psychoanalytic
Implications of Recent Research on Sleep and Dreaming", Journal of the
American Psychoanalytic Association 13, no.2 (April 1965): 197 -303.

Chapter 2

1   From Gillian Holloway's website. Gillian Holloway, Ph.D. www.lifetreks.com
2   Geoffrey A. Dudley, How to Understand Your Dreams, published by Melvin
Powers Whilshire Books Company 1957 California, printed by Hal Leighton
Printing Company, North California Pg 48

3   Geoffrey A. Dudley, *How to Understand Your Dreams*, published by Melvin Powers Whilshire Books Company 1957 California, printed by Hal Leighton Printing Company, North California Pg 50

4   James Ryle. *"A Dream Come True"*, Creation House now called Charisma House House Publishers 1995. Page 54
     I recommend you obtain this book and in particular refer to chapter three, Sleep Fancies & Other Vain Imaginations where James Ryle identifies 6 ways to recognise false dreams and visions. His whole book makes excellent reading, as well as 'Hippo in the Garden' also authored by James Ryle and published by Creation House.

5   James Ryle. *"A Dream Come True"*, Creation House now called Charisma House Publishers 1995. Page 35 – 36.

6   Simon J. Kistemaker, *Exposition of the Acts of the Apostles* Grand Rapids, Mich:Baker Bookhouse, 1990 Page 89.

7   John Peter Lange, *The Gospel According to John*. New York: Charles Scribners Sons, 1884. Page 48.

8   J.M. Lower, ed. *The Zondervan Pictorial Encyclopaedia of the Bible* Grand Rapids Mich Zondervan Publishing House, 1975. Vol. 2. Page 890.

9   James Ryle. *"A Dream Come True"*, Creation House now called Charisma House Publishers 1995. Page 15.

10   Charles Spurgeon. Metropolitan Tabernacle Pulpit. Carlisle Pa: The Banner of Truth, 1991. vol 14. Sermon # 806.

Chapter 3

1   Jane Hamon, *Dreams and Visions*, (Published by Regal Books a Division of Gospel Light/Regal Books. Ventura California, USA93003) 2000. Page 45. Used by permission.
     A very practical and easy to read book, Jane Hamon cuts through the psychological mumbo-jumbo to give a clear biblical understanding of the language of dreams.

2   Geoffrey A. Dudley, *How to Understand Your Dreams*, published by Melvin Powers Whilshire Books Company 1957 California, printed by Hal Leighton Printing Company, North California Pg 11-12

3   Spurgeon's Dream. I heard it used as a point of reference to a preacher's message when visiting our church.

4   Jim Rohn, Businessman, Entrepreneur, Motivational Communicator and author of many self help books. Truly one of the great minds of the modern era.

5   Quotation taken from: Bible Illustrator Version 3 Delux for Windows 1998, Parsons Technology, Hiawatha, Iowa U.S.A.

6   James Ryle. As cited in *"A Dream Ccome Ttrue"*, Creation House now called Charisma House Publishers Publishers 1995. Page 131 - 133. Full account of Ward Hill Lamon records on Abraham Lincoln's Dream.

Chapter 4

1   Ann Spangler. Dreams: *Miracles Can Happen in the Middle of the Night*. Grand Rapids, Michigan. Zondervan Publishing House. 1997. Page 18.

2   Herman H. Riffel, Dreams: *Giants and Geniuses in the Making*, Destiny Image Publishers. 1996. Page 23.

3   Herman H. Riffel, *Dream Interpretation 'A Biblical Understanding'*, 1993, Pg 40 Destiny Image Publishers 1993, 167 Walnut Bottom Road, Shippensburg, PA 17257. www.destinyimage.com
     Herman Riffel an ordained Baptist minister and graduate of the Multnomah School of the Bible, Wheaton College has done extensive study on dreams at the Jung Institute in Zurich, Switzerland. In this book he deals with the purpose and importance of dreams and introduces the reader to the language of symbols.

4   As cited in The Holy Bible, New International Version Study Bible, Copyright 1973, 1978, 1984 by International Bible Society. Used by permission of Zondervan Publishing House 1985, Pg 1570 -1571

Chapter 5

1   Ira Milligan, *Understanding the Dreams You Dream*, 1993, Pg 3. Used by permission of (Destiny Image Publishers, 167 Walnut Bottom Road, Shippensburg, PA 17257. www.destinyimage.com Inc 1997)

2   Benney Thomas, *Exploring the World of Dreams*, (Whitaker House U.S.A. 1990) Pg 145 –146

3   Morton Kelsey, Dreams: A Way to Listen to God, : 1989, Page 52. Publisher Paulist Press, Inc., New York/Mahwah, N.J. Used with permission of Paulist Press. www.paulistpress.com

Chapter 6

1   Paul Youngi Cho, *The Fourth Dimension*, (Logos International, Plainfield, New Jersey U.S.A. 1979) pg 44
2   An easy to read article in Psychology Today, September Edition 1999, 'Dreaming Up a Good Mood", refers to research on the effect that moods and emotions have in dreams conducted by Rosalind Cartwright, Ph.D. Director of the Sleep Research Centre at Rush-Presbyterian-St. Luke's Medical Centre in Chicago. The article looks at how depression affects dreams and how dreams affect depression.

Chapter 7

1   Anna Faraday, *The Dream Game*, (Published in Great Britain by Maurice Temple Smith Ltd 1975, 1974 AFAR PUBLICATIONS) pg 76-77,
2   Jeremy Taylor, Dream Work: *Techniques For Discovering the Creative Power of Dreams*, (Published by Paulist Press, New Jersey U.S.A Pg 65
3   Herman Riffel, *Your Dreams: God's Neglected Gift*, (Printed in Great Britain for Kingsway Publications Ltd 1981) Pg 62
4   Herman Riffel, *Your Dreams: God's Neglected Gift*, (Printed in Great Britain for Kingsway Publications Ltd 1981) Pg 63
5   Anna Faraday, *The Dream Game*, (Published in Great Britain by Maurice Temple Smith Ltd 1975, 1974 AFAR PUBLICATIONS) pg 85

Chapter 8

1   Herman H. Riffel, *Dreams: Giants and Geniuses in the Making*, Destiny Image Publishers. 1996. Page 4
2   *The Grossett Webster Dictionary*, Edited by: Charles P. Chadsey & Harold Wentworth, Publishers Grossett & Dunlap, New York U.S.A. 1974
3   I owe much of my understanding of the use of puns in dreams to Anna Faraday's work. A more detailed and comprehensive understanding of this area can be found in her book: '*The Dream Game*', chapter 6, (Published in Great Britain by Maurice Temple Smith Ltd 1975) pg 85

Chapter 9

1   Valerie Moolan, *The Meaning of Your Dreams*, Castle Books, New York 1969., This edition published with the arrangement of Cornerstone Library, Pg 18

2   Dr. Hartmann, professor of psychiatry from Tufts University School of Medicine, and director, Sleep Disorders Centre, Newton-Wellesley Hospital, Boston, Mass., is the author of Dreams and Nightmares: In The USA TODAY, March Edition 1999, 'The Nature and Uses of Dreaming' Dr Hartmann gives some helpful insight into stress and trauma and how they are connected to our dreams. His research and years of study help identify why certain nightmares may take place.

Chapter 10

1   Rick Joyner, A Prophetic Vision for the 21st Century, (Thomas Nelson Publishers Inc, Nashville, Tennessee U.S.A. 1995) 1999, Chapter 6, Page 86. Excerpts used by permission, Morning Star Fellowship Church,website: www.morningstarministries.org

2   Benney Hinn, *Good Morning Holy Spirit*, (Reproduced and printed in Great Britain for Word U.K. Ltd by Cox & Wyman ltd 1991) First Published in U.S.A by Thomas Nelson Publishers Inc, Nashville Tennessee U.S.A.

3   James Ryle. "*A Dream Come True*", Creation House now called Charisma House Publishers Publishers 1995. Page 102.

4   Story taken from the Open Doors USA website - https://www.opendoorsusa.org/takeaction/pray/tag-prayer-updates-post/after-dreams-of-jesus-imam-renounces-islam/ Used with permission: www.OpenDoorsUSA.org

OTHER RESOURCES

For further information on Zoran Paunovich's ministry and resources please refer to his website
www.zoranpaunovich.com